Praise for *The Mystery of the Cross*

"Carefully researched, *The Mystery of the Cross* . . . [allows] us to see this basic, simple symbol of crossed wooden beams as both analogy and actuality. The cross stands for all that Jesus did and does for the faithful—a theme emphasized in this outstanding book."

Luci Shaw, author of *The Crime of Living Cautiously* and Writer in Residence, Regent College

"With our imaginations being blasted by advertising brands and erotic innuendo, we need this book's authentic images of faith. A treasure in itself, it documents how centuries of brothers and sisters in the faith have bound their thoughts to our self-giving Christ."

Jan Johnson, author of *Spiritual Disciplines Companion*

"Nourishment for the mind as well as the soul. . . . Mystery indeed; this book reveals truths on multiple levels."

Marshall Shelley, vice president, Christianity Today International

"You hold a jewel in your hands. In this book, Judith explores through the ages and the arts the beauty and mystery of the cross. This will not be a one-time read but a book that I believe will enrich your devotional life for years to come."

Sheila Walsh, author of *Beautiful Things Happen When a Woman Trusts God*

"Through story and art, Judith weaves a tapestry in this book that will do more than merely inform us. We will be inspired by the mystery and transformed by the message!"

Stephen W. Smith, author of *The Lazarus Life*

"Judith Couchman has compiled a challenging historical record of an earlier church integrating the cross, both symbolically and sacramentally, into worship, into daily living and into personal devotion. If the measure of a book is how much it impacts our thinking after the pages are closed, *The Mystery of the Cross* has caused me to reconsider how I can better employ representations of this iconic image every day in every way."

Karen Mains, author of *Open Heart—Open Home*

"Judith Couchman has given us a remarkably rich tour of the history of the cross. She traces the journey of this centrally important Christian symbol from its earliest pre-Christian origins to the present in a series of short, engaging chapters. Through this the reader is drawn into the transformational power and glory of Christ's death and resurrection. The result is a book I highly recommend."

Juliet Benner, *Conversations* art director

"Prompted by the author's own discovery of the cross in Christian art, these short devotional essays will help others to encounter and better understand the complex and fascinating history of this powerful symbol—throughout history and in their own lives."

Robin M. Jensen, author of *Understanding Early Christian Art*

"Judith Couchman uses various art images from the past two millennia to tell stories and teach truths about the cross, many of which were entirely new to me. But more, she not only informs but also inspires the reader. Her book is both fresh and refreshing, new and renewing."

Gerald L. Sittser, author of *A Grace Disguised* and *Water from a Deep Well*

THE MYSTERY
OF THE CROSS

Bringing Ancient
Christian Images to Life

JUDITH COUCHMAN

IVP Books

An imprint of InterVarsity Press
Downers Grove, Illinois

InterVarsity Press
P.O. Box 1400, Downers Grove, IL 60515-1426
World Wide Web: www.ivpress.com
E-mail: email@ivpress.com

InterVarsity Press® is the book-publishing division of InterVarsity Christian Fellowship/USA®, a movement of students and faculty active on campus at hundreds of universities, colleges and schools of nursing in the United States of America, and a member movement of the International Fellowship of Evangelical Students. For information about local and regional activities, write Public Relations Dept., InterVarsity Christian Fellowship/USA, 6400 Schroeder Rd., P.O. Box 7895, Madison, WI 53707-7895, or visit the IVCF website at <www.intervarsity.org>.

All Scripture quotations, unless otherwise indicated, are taken from the Holy Bible, New International Version®. NIV®. Copyright ©1973, 1978, 1984 by International Bible Society. Used by permission of Zondervan Publishing House. All rights reserved.

Design: Cindy Kiple
Cover Image: Cross of Sbeitla, from the Basilica of Henchir Ali Ben Rzal, Tunisia at Musee National du Bardo, Le Bardo, Tunisia. Lauros/Giraudon/The Bridgeman Art Library
Interior chapter illustrations: Anne Elhajoui

Interior photos: Aerial photo of the standing stone of Callanish in chapter one is used by permission of D. W. Harding. Photo of the Passion Sarcophagus in chapter three is used by permission of Allan T. Kohl and Art Images for College Teaching/AICT <www.arthist.umn.edu/aict/html/>. Photo of the Jonah fresco from the Catacomb of Callixtus in chapter thirteen is used by permission of Pontificia Commissione di Archeologia Sacra. Photo of St. Catherine's Monastery used in chapter nineteen, ©Argenberg <www.argenberg.com/album> or <www.flickr.com/photos/argenberg/134947647>. Photo of the oil lamps with crosses used in chapter twenty-two, ©The Israel Museum, by Avraham Hay. Photo of the baptismal font in a fifth-century church in Shivta, used in chapter twenty-nine, is taken from Wikimedia Commons/Eitan f. Photo of the bread stamps with crosses used in chapter thirty, ©The Israel Museum, by Avraham Hay. Photo of the ninth-century Khludov Psalter used in chapter thirty-three is taken from Wikimedia Commons. Photo of the Hill of Crosses in chapter forty is used by permission of Kim Stephenson.

ISBN 978-0-8308-3539-3

Printed in the United States of America ∞

Library of Congress Cataloging-in-Publication Data

Couchman, Judith, 1953-
  The mystery of the cross: bringing ancient Christian images to life
  /Judith Couchman.
      p. cm.
  Includes bibliographical references.
  ISBN 978-0-8308-3539-3 (pbk.: alk. paper)
  1. Jesus Christ—Crucifixion. I. Title.
  BT453.C67 2009
  246'.558—dc22

                                                                                          2009031645

P	18	17	16	15	14	13	12	11	10	9	8	7	6	5	4	3	2	1
Y	24	23	22	21	20	19	18	17	16	15	14	13	12	11	10	09

In memory of Opal,
my beloved mother and friend.

Contents

Part Seven: Enduring Mysteries

Acknowledgments

Many thanks to my friends and family who supported me while researching and writing this book, plunging into new territory with the audacity of an explorer. Beth, Donna, Laurel and Melinda, thanks for the lively talks in cafes and coffee shops. Kathe, our weekly phone conversations kept me motivated. Mary, thanks for always offering me grace. Latayne, I'm humbled by your practical support, and the writing retreat with the three docs cheered me during a low point. Anne, Beth, Lucky, Nancy and Shirley: I appreciated and depended on your prayers.

The Munro clan—Matt, Mel, Claire, Kendra, Kaelyn and Oliver—wrapped me in family affection, greeting me with hugs and doggie kisses after emerging from my writing cave. Most poignantly, my loving mother consistently affirmed me. A day before Mom slipped into a coma and died, she still asked about my writing projects, even though she could barely talk. I will always remember those words.

Two university professors, Suzanne and Elissa, unwittingly contributed to my work on this manuscript. By inviting me to teach online for the University of Colorado at Colorado Springs, they opened a gate to study, research and teaching that fed facts, stories and fresh ideas into my knowledge of early Christian art. Thanks for the ongoing adventure in art history.

I'm especially grateful that my friend Anne Elhajoui created the illustrations for this book; that Cindy Kiple designed a lovely cover; and that my editor, Cindy Bunch, waited during a writing stall when life served up six deaths in one year. As a young adult, I fantasized about becoming an IVP author. Dreams can come true.

Introduction

Christianity is a religion founded on
the mystery of the cross of Christ.

POPE LEO THE GREAT

THE ANCIENT BYZANTINE ARTISTS OF Eastern Christianity contributed a spectacular art form to church history by creating mosaics of biblical characters and stories, along with Christian signs and saints. Mosaicists pieced together tesserae (small pieces of stone, marble or glass) to create enormous images on church walls, ceilings and floors. Visiting a Byzantine church merits constant neck craning, looking up and down, at these intricate creations.

In the sixth century Archbishop Maximianus consecrated Ravenna, Italy's new basilica, Sant'Apollinare in Classe. He named the building after Saint Apollinare, an early martyr and the first Bishop of Ravenna, allegedly appointed by the apostle Peter himself. Walking up the nave, visitors gaze increasingly upward as they approach the apse image of Apollinare with outstretched arms, flanked by the sheep of Christ's flock. The mosaic is a fitting tribute to a holy man who endured repeated beatings for his faith and persistent ministry to Christians.

However, a dominant image looms above the revered bishop, indicating its preeminence. It's a large, gemmed cross with a small bust portrait of Christ positioned at the axis. Perhaps the mosaic's designer wanted to remind worshipers that even our most devout service can't compare to Christ's sacrificial victory. He wanted us to remember the meaning of the cross.

Early Christians and the Cross

When I began studying early Christian art at mid-life, I discovered how much ancient believers revered Christ's cross. They felt compelled to touch, honor and memorialize it. Christians passed along stories about its power, history and mystery. They replicated the cross in humble homes and grand basilicas, on catacomb walls and stone sarcophagi. Still, they knew the Savior, not the actual cross itself, had ushered in salvation and radically changed their lives. The sign of the cross prompted them to remember, follow and glorify the Lord. This simple sign increased their devotion to Christ.

As obvious as this cross appreciation seems, as a Protestant I hadn't encountered many of the long-established art, signs, legends, rituals, festivals and extra-biblical stories related to Christ's cross. Not because I didn't care; for the most part, I didn't know they existed. My church tradition hadn't taught them. As I sat in the classroom and studied at home, I thought: *This is fascinating. Has this information been here all along? Why haven't I heard about this?* I had lots of catching up to do. I wanted to understand the breadth of early Christianity and its relationship to the cross, the faith's core and widely known symbol.

As I researched and studied further, art and history about the cross both inspired and surprised me. The horror and audacity, simplicity and splendor, reverence and sincerity, captured my imagination. Early Christians so honored the cross, Byzantine religious leaders banned its image in floor mosaics so it wouldn't be stepped on. Somewhere in church history we'd misplaced this sacredness, and perhaps the earliest Christians guarded what we've now lost. On the other hand, certain stories and practices stretched me too far. I couldn't believe the superstitions or every extra-biblical story. Nor could I condone later abuses that pedaled the cross for money and miracles. Then and now, kitschy crosses outnumbered the liturgical ones. Still, somewhere in between, early Christians taught me remarkable, life-changing lessons about the cross.

When I shared these sign-of-the-cross anecdotes with my friends and family, they usually responded by saying, "I didn't know that." Or, "It's interesting. Tell me more." As a result, I wrote *The Mystery of the Cross*. It begins by addressing pre-Christian crosses and then the cross-related art, life and worship of early believers during the first millennium after Christ's birth. The chapters are both informational and devotional, prompting you to consider not just the early Christians, but the cross's influence on you, too.

Ancient Cross, Contemporary Life

If you haven't considered the cross beyond weekend worship, tapping into these images and stories can broaden and deepen, renew or strengthen your commitment to Christ. Exploring the art, uses and history of the cross can validate its centrality to the Christian faith. Meditating on its enduring meaning can help apply its power and principles to everyday matters.

Accordingly, *The Mystery of the Cross* invites you to read intriguing stories about the sign of the cross, ponder their meaning and consider how these anecdotes speak to you. The forty short chapters can be read for art appreciation, historical information, personal meditation, spiritual formation, small-group discussion, Lenten observation or worship insights. Whatever the use, *The Mystery of the Cross* can help you understand and appreciate the cross's spiritual work in the world and its power for everyday life.

Most of all, I hope this book witnesses mystery. The apostle Paul wrote about the gospel's mystery, revealed through Christ and his death on the cross. Irenaeus, a second-century church father, described it when he explained, "By means of a tree, we were made debtors to God. Likewise, by means of a tree [the cross], we can obtain the remission of our debt." Beyond glorious art, ancient history and intriguing anecdotes, the cross stands as a symbol of salvation. For reasons beyond my comprehension, the mighty God stooped to conquer evil and forgive sin. This is his eternal commitment. This is the inexpressible value and mystery of the cross.

PART ONE

Ancient Echoes of Christ

The Cross in Pre-Christian Times

From its simplicity of form, the cross has been used both as a religious symbol and as an ornament, from the dawn of . . . civilization. Various objects, dating from periods long anterior to the Christian era, have been found, marked with crosses of different designs, in almost every part of the old world. India, Syria, Persia, and Egypt have all yielded numerous examples, with numerous instances, dating from the later Stone Age to Christian times, have been found in every part of Europe.

THE ENCYCLOPEDIA BRITANNICA,

11TH EDITION

1

The Mystery of the Megalith

[He is able] to establish you . . . according to the revelation of the
mystery hidden for long ages past, but now revealed and made known
through the prophetic writings by the command of the eternal God,
so that all nations might believe and obey him. —ROMANS 16:25-26

The Standing Stones of Callanish

IF YOU DON'T MIND GRAY SKIES AND misty bogs, you can wander
through one of the world's intriguing mysteries. It's a group of huge,
upright stones, weathered and woodlike, but still erect after five thousand years in the Scottish Islands. In the nineteenth century peat dig-
gers excavated the isolated monument after falling leaves from a dozen
centuries halfway buried it in decayed vegetation. The stones stood so
intact that archaeologists didn't need to restore the ancient assemblage, except for straightening up one fallen stone.

So why are these stones significant?

With almost a thousand stone circles in the British Isles, only these
stones, the Standing Stones of Callanish, configure into a cross. Thir-

The Standing Stones of Callanish. Isle of Lewis, Scotland. 3000 to 2300 BC.

teen menhirs (upright stones) form a circle only twenty-two feet across, with additional stones radiating to the north, south, east and west in rows. The inner circle features a sunken grave, probably added hundreds of years after the monument's creation. Given the grouping's size and shape, Callanish is the second greatest megalith site in the world after Stonehenge in southern England. Viewed from above, the formation looks like a Celtic cross.

Scottish Legends and Stones

Several legends developed to explain the creation of this mysterious stone pattern. One story claimed when the ancient inhabitants on Lewis Island refused to convert to Christianity, the usually friendly Saint Kieran, an Irish monk, turned them into these stones. Another legend insisted the stones were people who'd sinned by playing on the Sabbath. A third tale promised that a marriage consummated within the inner circle would be a happy one. (During the nineteenth century the site hosted weddings.) Yet another story explained that during a famine, several women visited the circle of stones each night, where a benevolent white sea cow filled their pails with milk. This satiated hunger until one night a witch showed up, milked the cow into a sieve, and both disappeared.

Scottish legends aside, contemporary archaeologists date this "Stonehenge of the North" long before Christianity. Sometime between 3000 and 2300 BC, Bronze Age people hauled huge slabs to a sloped ridge overlooking the waters of Loch Roag on the west coast of Lewis Island. One of the first mentions of the Callanish stones in literature noted the enormity of this task. In the seventeenth century John Morrison, a resident of Lewis, mentioned the stones in "Description of the Lewis." He wrote, "In severall [sic] places there are great stones standing up straight in ranks, some two or three thick and 10, 12, and 15 foot high; It is left by traditione [sic] that these were a sort of men converted into stones by ane [sic] Inchanter [sic] . . . it cannot but be admired how they could be carried here."

Based on the Bronze Age time frame, a late nineteenth century theory suggested an astrological purpose for the stones: they aligned with the sun, moon, stars and horizon, helping to predict solstices or eclipses. But nobody knows for sure. One writer observed, "Callanish keeps its secrets." The stones shaped into a cross remain a mystery.

It's intriguing that thousands of years before Christ's death—as early as the Stone Age—the cross had already implanted its lasting mark on the earth. Ancient civilizations adopted this simple sign into their cultures and observances, evidenced by the artifacts left behind and dug up centuries or millennia later. But grappling experts can't always pinpoint these crosses' exact use or meaning. Sometimes researchers can only surmise, gripped and defeated by the enigma.

When the cross transitioned into Christianity's central identity, it burgeoned into the most recognizable sign in the world. But even today the cross, like a battered megalith, shields a mystery. From all the infinite possibilities, why did God choose this common formation, this pre-owned symbol, to assure our salvation? We can only wonder.

God keeps his secrets, too.

A Mystery That Saves Us

When we encounter the sign of the cross in pre-Christian cultures, we gaze at mystery. Scholars of many stripes want to learn more about this ancient mark: its use, its creators, its meaning. But often history locks these facts in the ravages of time. Earthbound, these seekers may never accomplish their goals. So why should we, the everyday followers of Christ, bother with a cross sign that predates him? Isn't knowledge about the Savior's cross and an assurance of its redemptive message enough?

Undoubtedly, Christ's cross is crucial. It's the instrument God chose to unveil "the mystery hidden for long ages past" (Rom 16:25), his plan of salvation. Through this cross, he initiated the death, burial and resurrection of his Son—the Passion cycle that leads us to spiritual freedom. Without this cross, we'd be stuck in our sin with no future hope of heaven. Without this cross, we couldn't pattern Christ's death-to-life transformation, the process of dying to ourselves and rising to new life in him. God could have chosen any method to save us, but he used the cross. The cross is our spiritual centerpiece, the sign of our soul's emancipation.

However, the pre-Christian cross might offer a sliver of insight to God. Some skeptics claim this ancient sign of the cross disproves Christianity. Because this image recurred in early divergent cultures, they claim Christ's story wasn't true; that the first Christians borrowed "the cross myth" and its sign from pre-existing religions. But couldn't the God who oversees the universe and its events have etched the cross image into humanity's soul before Christ appeared? Could this early sign have prophesied our need for a savior? Perhaps when the pagan ancients created their own gods and religious signs, they unwittingly patterned the way of Christ.

It's an idea I've pondered: Before Jesus appeared, the pre-Christian cross foretold his arrival. This cross reminds me of God's plan—the mystery hidden through the ages—to rescue us from eternal death. The apostle Paul wrote about "the mystery of Christ, which was not made known to men in other generations as it has now been revealed by the Spirit to God's holy apostles and prophets. This mystery is that through the gospel the Gentiles are heirs together with Israel, members together of one body, and sharers together in the promise in Christ Jesus" (Eph 3:4-6).

What a wonder. Before time began, God planned to rescue us.

2

Egyptian Signs of Life

For God so loved the world that he gave his one and only Son, that whoever believes in him shall not perish but have eternal life. —JOHN 3:16

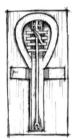

King Tut's *Ankh* Mirror

EACH MORNING, AN EGYPTIAN PRIEST respectfully greeted an image of Amun with the blessing "May you awake in peace!" hoping this god of fertility would wake up in a good mood. The Egyptians believed Amun and other gods could alter fate, so priests tended to all their "needs." Consequently, every morning, in every Egyptian temple, priests performed a sacred ritual.

Entering the dark, inner chamber of the temple, a priest lit a flare, broke the seal on the inner sanctum's door, and announced to the sculptured god: "Truly, I am a servant of god . . . the king . . . sends me to look at the god. I am come to do what may be done." After this introduction, the priest burned incense, cleaned and applied fresh makeup to the statue, and anointed it with ten different oils. He then "awakened" the god, closed the door and resealed it. As the priest departed, he wiped away traces of his footsteps and extinguished the flame, knowing he'd reenact this ceremony the next morning.

The priest completed the ritual carefully, hoping to avoid chaos within Egypt. He believed if anyone neglected this duty, calamity would inflict the land. The gods would turn angry and depart, leaving the kingdom "full of tombs and corpses."

According to tradition, the gods had designated Egypt's ruler to conduct this holy ritual. But no busy pharaoh could be everywhere at once, so he assigned these duties to priests in temples across the nation. He only attended the ceremony at one location on feast days, yet the walls of many Egyptian temples painted the pharaoh as the sole keeper of the morning ritual. In these images he prayed, burned incense, offered sacrifices, presented gifts and served milk or wine to a god. These acts assuaged the menacing uraeus, an arching serpent on the god's headdress. In return, the god handed the pharaoh an *ankh,* the symbol of life. Hieroglyphs on the walls exclaimed, "I give you life, goodness and health ever more."

The Cross with a Loop

In ancient Egypt the *ankh* frequently appeared in that kingdom's art, religion and royal life. It resembled a cross with a loop on top, and scholars have debated the rounded part's specific meaning. They've suggested everything from a sandal strap to the sunrise to a sexual union. In Egyptian art the gods carried the *ankh,* and it's widely accepted that the symbol represented both life on earth and in the netherworld.

To promote a pharaoh's image, paintings and relief sculptures (raised carvings on flat surfaces) on royal walls often depicted gods bestowing *ankhs* on a ruler. For example, an entrance to King Sahure's funerary temple at Abusir incorporated long rows of gods offering the life-giving symbols to this Fifth Dynasty ruler (c. 2458-2446 BC), reaffirming their allegiance to him. Large hieroglyphs proclaimed, "We give you all life, stability and dominion, all joy, all offerings, all per-

fect things that are in Upper Egypt, since you have appeared as king of
Upper and Lower Egypt alive forever." Not far away, a relief sculpture
in the temple of Niuserre showed Anubis, god of the dead, filling the
pharaoh's mouth and hands with *ankhs,* infusing the king with the
"breath of life."

The gods also poured *ankhs* over monarchs, representing the regen-
erating power of water. In response to this metaphor, artisans molded
libation vessels for sacred ceremonies into the *ankh* shape. Undoubtedly, no other symbol appeared as frequently in the Egyptian world,
from small manufactured objects to the walls, shrines and pillars of
royal and sacred architecture. The *ankh* represented the gift of life,
the blessing of a good life and hope for the afterlife.

Mirroring Life and Death

Despite the *ankh's* widespread reputation as a symbol of life, in the
Egyptian language it played a double role. A hand mirror *(maw her)*
meant "that which sees the face," but this grooming aid, usually owned
by the upper classes, was also called an *ankh.* A mirror designed in the
shape of an *ankh,* like the elaborate one discovered in King Tutankhamun's tomb in the Valley of the Kings, pointed to life after death.
King Tut might have used this mirror during his lifetime, but it's more
plausible that artisans created it for his burial. During the Middle
Kingdom (c. 2040-1640 BC) artists often painted mirrors on wooden
coffins, intended for the deceased's use in the afterlife. Sometimes a
mirror nestled beneath the mummy's wrappings, under the head or
on the face. *Ankh*-shaped mirrors carved for tombs inextricably linked
life and death together, reminding Egyptians of their frailties and ultimate destination.

Eventually the Copts—early Christians and descendents of the an-
cient Egyptians—adopted the *ankh* sign as their Christian cross. The
Coptic Church called it the *crux ansata,* the handled or "eyed" cross.
Turning away from Egypt's pagan beliefs, the Copts redeemed the

ankh's meaning. They celebrated the life-giving message of the Christian cross, with Christ as the life giver. In the fourth-century Coptic Liturgy According to Saint Basil, early Christian Egyptians acknowledged the Lord as "the forgiveness of our sins, the light of our souls, *our life,* and our strength and our confidence" (italics added). Like the *ankh* mirror with its double meaning, these worshipers believed in the paradox of the Christian cross. Two wooden beams that proclaimed death also became a symbol of eternal life.

This paradox reaches through the ages and claims me, too. In a visit to the British Museum I couldn't leave without stopping in the gift shop, a faithful ritual I keep when exploring art exhibits. Thoroughly looking through the books and replicas, I felt drawn to a necklace—a black ribbon with a silver *ankh* dangling from it. *Ah, small enough to stuff in my suitcase,* I thought, satisfying my sense of entitlement toward museum souvenirs. I've owned the necklace for a few years, but ironically, I've never worn it. The black ribbon is too short to wear comfortably, but even if I attached a longer ribbon or chain, I'd worry that people might mistakenly assume I'm promoting Egyptian paganism. Every so often, though, I pull it out and think about the *crux ansata,* the Copts and how they transformed a pagan symbol into a sign of Christ's cross.

I also remember that Christ's cross represents both death and life. I marvel at this dual sacred meaning. But even more, I can believe. With the ancient Copts and their liturgy, I can pray and affirm that Christ's body was sacrificed "for salvation, remission of sins and eternal life to those who partake of him. I believe, I believe, I believe that this is so in truth. Amen."

3

The Healing Cross

As Moses lifted up the snake in the desert, so the
Son of Man must be lifted up, that everyone who believes
in him may have eternal life. —JOHN 3:14-15

The Healing Cross

In the Old Testament God didn't suffer fools gladly.

When the Israelites tromped from Mount Hor toward the Red Sea, they grew impatient and griped about a lack of provision. They complained to Moses, "Why have you brought us up out of Egypt to die in the desert? There is no bread! There is no water! And we detest this miserable food!" (Num 21:5). Foolishness mixed into the complaint because not long before, God had spilled water from an impenetrable rock to quench their thirst, even though Moses hadn't followed God's instructions carefully (Num 20:11). Evidently, nobody had learned from that experience.

The Israelites complained so much, the Old Testament says God infiltrated poisonous snakes among them and many people died, writhing along with the serpents. Soon the terrified survivors admitted their sin to Moses, asking him to pray for the Lord to withdraw the snakes. "We sinned when we spoke against the LORD and against you. Pray that the LORD will take the snakes away from us," they cried, suddenly feeling like fools (Num. 21:7). This time a more mindful Moses followed God's instructions exactly. He crafted a bronze snake and attached it to a pole. Anyone bitten by a snake could look at the image and survive (Num 21:6-9). The Old Testament account doesn't say whether the Jews actually focused on the snake; the text just assumes they did. Who would be foolish enough not to look and live?

Healing and Mythology

Throughout Scripture, God redeemed his people with metaphors and sometimes irony. In Israel's Desert of Zin the snake—associated with sin, evil, death and deception—transformed into a healing balm midst a wasteland. The serpent served as a powerful metaphor in other ancient cultures, too, sometimes incorporating the reference to healers and healing.

Greek mythology assimilated the snake-and-pole symbolism into its stories about Asclepius, the god of medicine and healing. According to mythology's timeline, he was born a mortal about a century after Jehovah dictated staking the snake-wrapped pole in the desert. A myth claims the centaur Chiron raised Asclepius, teaching him about surgery, drugs, incantations and love potions. Later the goddess Athena handed him a vial of blood that could raise people from the dead. Eventually Zeus, the supreme ruler of the gods, killed Asclepius with a thunderbolt, punishing the healer for interfering with the world's natural order by performing resurrections. After his death, the gods awarded Asclepius immorality as the constellation Ophiuchus, which means "serpent bearer."

The Greeks adopted Asclepius as their god of medicine and healing, and believed that during the Trojan War, he healed the hero

Philoctetes from a snake bite. In artwork, Asclepius often holds a snake-entwined staff, like the free-standing marble sculptures in the Louvre Museum in Paris and the National Archaeological Museum in Athens. In these sculptures and other depictions of Asclepius, his muscled body exudes health, power and confidence.

Around 300 BC, the cult of Asclepius escalated, with pilgrims traveling to his temples for healing. To honor this god, Greek priests used serpents in healing rituals and doctors allowed non-poisonous snakes to crawl around dormitories of the sick and injured. But despite the widespread popularity of Asclepius for several centuries, Jews and early Christians took no stock in the mythical god's motionless pole and snake. For them, Asclepius couldn't compare to Jehovah, the true God of Israel who offered authentic forgiveness, healing and eternal life.

The Snake and the Cross

Over a millennia after Moses raised a pole in the desert, a member of the Jewish ruling council clandestinely visited a controversial healer. Except on this occasion the questioning Nicodemus sought healing for his soul. Jesus explained the way to salvation, comparing himself to the ancient bronze serpent. He told Nicodemus, "As Moses lifted up the snake in the desert, so the Son of Man must be lifted up, that everyone who believes in him may have eternal life" (Jn 3:14-15). With this metaphor, Jesus established the desert pole as a forerunner to his cross.

The third-century apologist, Tertullian of Carthage, expanded the snake comparison further. "Why did . . . Moses . . . exhibit a bronze serpent, placed on a tree?" he asked rhetorically. "Is it not that in this case he was exhibiting the Lord's cross on which the serpent, the devil, was defeated?" In the fourth century John Chrysostom, the archbishop of Constantinople, also elaborated on the snake-cross comparison. Like Tertullian, he began with a question: "Seest thou the cause of the Crucifixion, and the salvation which is by it? Seest thou the relationship of the type to the reality? there the Jews escaped death, but the temporal, here believers the eternal; there the hanging serpent healed the bites of serpents, here the Crucified Jesus cured the wounds inflicted by the spiritual dragon [another name for serpent]; there he who looked with his bodily eyes was healed, here he who beholds with the eyes of his understanding puts off all his sins."

These church fathers emphasized the powerful salvation image of the snake-wrapped pole. Through this sign of the cross, they recalled the Savior's victory over Satan. With this metaphor, they affirmed that Christ's death and resurrection offered forgiveness and healing. Eventually, for Christians an image of the cross with a snake wrapped around it became known as the healing cross. We still recognize this sign of the cross today, either in the shape of a Latin cross with crossbeams, or a Tau cross shaped like a "T." We can still look up to a God who forgives and heals.

On the other hand, the healing cross can disconcert us. Although I'm fascinated by the many cross signs that developed through the centuries, I'm uneasy looking at a pole with a serpent hanging from it. I'm conditioned to think of a snake as sly, unreliable and posed to bite; the personification of Satan in the Garden of Eden. I can barely look at a snake without feeling anxious, even if it's only an image in an art book. So it's hard to think of this slithering reptile as a representation of God's desire to forgive my sin and to heal me, body and soul. I want images of Jesus as the searching Shepherd or the gentle Lamb of God to remind me of that, not a belly-crawling snake.

Yet again, isn't that just like God? He converts bad into good. He uses the everyday metaphors, the unexpected events, the least likely people and creeping creatures to communicate his life-saving message. He even startles us to get our attention. He wants us to look and live.

4

Ugly Roman Power Symbols

Being found in appearance as a man he humbled himself and became
obedient to death—even death on a cross! —PHILIPPIANS 2:8

The Latin Cross

THE ROMAN STOIC PHILOSOPHER SENECA preferred committing suicide to enduring crucifixion's abasement. Seneca's revelation in a letter to his student-friend Lucilius indicates the dread, pain and humiliation of first-century crucifixion. Though the Roman Empire permitted suicide, but it wasn't considered an honorable way to die.

In the Roman world, crucifixion ranked as the worst possible death due to its prolonged agony, and because authorities reserved crucifixion for the lowest forms of humanity: the criminals, the slaves, the rebels, the enemies. Authorities often crucified victims in public places as power symbols and deterrents to bad behaviors and imperial opposition. The cross, a pagan symbol, stood as the greatest public shame.

Jews understood the explicit horrors of crucifixion. For them, it meant the abandonment of God cursing them (Deut 21:23). The first-century Jewish historian Josephus called the cross "a most miserable death." Although Jewish history included both crucifying others and being crucified, the Jews seldom crucified, especially compared to the massive crucifixions conducted by warring pagans.

When the Romans plundered Jerusalem in 70 AD, the Emperor Titus scared Jews into submission by condoning crucifixions. Josephus wrote that "the soldiers out of the wrath and hatred they bore the Jews, nailed those they caught, one after one way, and another after another, to the crosses, by way of jest, when their multitude was so great, that room was wanting for the crosses, and crosses wanting for the bodies." Also in the first century, the Emperor Caligula tortured and crucified Jews to entertain the people of Alexandria, Egypt. Before that, in the first century BC, the Maccabean Alexander Jannaeus crucified eight hundred Pharisees after stopping a revolt near Samaria in Israel. But mass crucifixions weren't just reserved for Jews. In the same century, the Romans crucified six thousand slaves involved in a revolt led by Spartacus. Soldiers set up the crosses along the Appian Way to quell additional revolts. After Tyre, Phoenicia (Lebanon), fell to the angry Alexander the Great in the fourth century BC, he ordered the crucifixions of two thousand military-aged men and sold thirty thousand others into slavery. Crucifixion satisfied the vengeful needs of emperors and other warring leaders.

Before the Emperor Constantine banned crucifixion in the fourth century, this death ritual spanned eight hundred years. For punishment, the Assyrians and Persians "practiced impalement (mounting a living body on a pointed stake)," but Persians also conducted crucifixions. Adding to the list, the Greeks, Phoenicians and Carthaginians also pounded crucifying wood into the ground as a punishment and a warning. Crucifixion underscored how ugly humanity's vengeful heart can be.

The Crucifixion Process

Most ancient secular writers omitted the horrible details when they addressed crucifixion. The Bible doesn't divulge the revolting specifics about Christ's crucifixion, either. However, by piecing together biblical and extrabiblical accounts, scholars offer varied opinions about Roman crucifixions in the early first century. While we don't know the procedure for mass crucifixions, enough information exists to describe the process for individuals and small groups. Most references to crucifixions focused on men.

After receiving a sentence of crucifixion, Roman soldiers tortured the condemned man, usually flogging him to a bloody pulp. Wearing a sign around his neck indicating his crime of sedition, the accused carried a crossbeam to the place of crucifixion, often near the location of his crime and along busy, public roads. As the man struggled toward his death, he passed crowds of jeering onlookers, acting like an informal, maniacal jury that reveled in his misery. To increase the shame, soldiers at the crucifixion site stripped off the victim's clothes. It's generally believed they tied or nailed his hands to the crossbeam. Then they inserted the crossbeam into an upright post and tied or nailed his feet to this vertical pole.

However, some historians disagree with this description of Christ's cross. Christ could have been nailed, with his hands over his head, to a *crux simplex* (an upright post with no cross beam). This was a common form of crucifixion until the ancient Phoenicians added a transverse beam to the post. Some scholars believe the Romans crucified Christ on an actual tree. Still others claim the *crux immissa,* the familiar Latin cross depicted in Western artwork. Altogether, it's possible that the form of crucifixion varied in the Roman Empire.

Researchers also disagree about how a crucified person died. Based on a body's position on the cross, the complicated debate has suggested a ruptured heart, asphyxiation (suffocation), and hypovolemic shock (a decrease in the amount of circulating blood). Some victims died within a few hours, but authorities preferred to prolong a death as a spectacle and deterrent to watchers. Whatever happened, it's unanimous that crucifixion humiliated and deprived a person in brutal physical and emotional pain.

"So they left the crucified one to die, the feet of the victim only a few inches from the ground, not high in the air," explains scholar Harold F. Vos. "He suffered greatly, including the taunts and indignities of passersby, and exposure to heat and cold and insects (and sometimes animals). He suffered the pain of wounds, often infected, and the intense thirst. Depending on the strength of one's constitution, death might be prolonged but usually took at least thirty-six hours. And then the body hung there to decay and to be devoured by scavenger birds." Or it was thrown on a garbage heap, deprived of a burial.

Our Unbloody Sacrifice

It's seems unconscionable that God submitted to the cross, a symbol that opposed his message of love and forgiveness. In the Roman world it represented paganism, cruelty, hatred, bondage and death. With humility, Christ faced down humanity's worst to give us God's best.

The medieval poem "Dream of the Rood" told the crucifixion story from the viewpoint of the rood (the cross), as if a Passion character capable of pain and grief. The rood describes how Christ's suffering shook all creation:

> The young hero stripped himself—he, God Almighty—
> strong and stout-minded. He mounted high gallows,
> bold before many, when he would loose mankind.
> I shook when that Man clasped me. I dared, still, not bow to earth,
> fall to earth's fields, but had to stand fast.
> Rood was I reared. I lifted a mighty King,
> Lord of the heavens, dared not to bend.
> With dark nails they drove me through: on me those sores are seen,

open malice-wounds. I dared not scathe anyone.
They mocked us both, we two together. All wet with blood I was,
poured out from that Man's side, after ghost he gave up.
Much have I born on that hill
of fierce fate. I saw the God of hosts
harshly stretched out. Darknesses had
wound round with clouds the corpse of the Wielder,
bright radiance; a shadow went forth,
dark under heaven. All creation wept,
King's fall lamented. Christ was on rood.

What do we offer to Christ in return? In the late fourth or early fifth century, the Liturgy of Saint James answered, "Making remembrance of his life-giving sufferings, his saving cross and death, his burial and resurrection on the third day from the dead, and his session at the right hand of You his God and Father, and his second glorious and fearful coming when he will judge the living and the dead . . . we offer to You O Lord, this awesome and unbloody sacrifice, beseeching You to deal with us not according to our sins . . . but according to Your great mercy and love."

Our most grateful, humble response to Christ's crucifixion doesn't compensate for his suffering. But God knew it never could.

PART TWO

The Pain and the Glory

The Cross and the Suffering Savior

According to tradition, [during the crucifixion] our Lord's back was turned toward Jerusalem, which was in the east and his face toward the west. This may have been a refinement of cruelty on the part of the executioners. Jesus' back was placed toward the capital of the nation of whom the Roman governor had written he was "King," and his face turned to the setting sun, not only to remind him of his departing glory, as his enemies fondly deemed, but that no torture, however petty, yet agonizing, as the blaze of the sun would be, might be spared.

WILLIAM WOOD SEYMOUR,

THE CROSS IN TRADITION, HISTORY, AND ART

5

Shouldering the Cross

*A certain man from Cyrene, Simon, the father of Alexander
and Rufus, was passing by on his way in from the country,
and they forced him to carry the cross.* —MARK 15:21

**Simon of Cyrene on
the Passion Sarcophagus**

DRAGGING A CROSS BEAM TOWARD GOLGOTHA, Jesus collapsed from
pain and exhaustion. It's no wonder. Before this journey, Luke tells us
"his sweat was like drops of blood" while praying in the Garden of
Gethsemane (Lk 22:44). Later officers struck, fist-beat and scourged
Jesus before crowning him with thorns. When he weakened and
couldn't shoulder the load, Roman officers pressed the bystander Simon of Cyrene to carry the rough-hewn beam to Golgotha, The Place
of the Skull.

The Gospel of Luke mentions that Simon was coming in from the
country (Lk 23:26), and most likely the sudden responsibility shocked
him. New Testament scholars conjecture that later Simon's sons, Rufus and Alexander, became well-known members of the Christian

congregation in Rome. Maybe they kept alive the story of an unsus-
pecting father groaning under the weight of their Savior's cross.

Eighteen centuries later, a Catholic nun published a Passion story
that memorialized Simon's poignant intervention on the Calvary road.
Anne Catherine Emmerich, though practically illiterate, dictated details about Christ's crucifixion that corroborated and augmented the
Bible's events. Anne claimed the stories emerged from her ecstatic vi-
sions, accompanied by physical torments. But in an introduction to
the *Dolorous Passion of Our Lord Jesus Christ* released in 1862, Anne's
publisher carefully stipulated that her stories were meditational rather
than historical. With this perspective, the *Dolorous Passion* can be read
like a historical novel, suggesting how shouldering the cross transformed Simon.

According to this nineteenth-century account, Simon was "a gardener, just returning home after working in a garden near the eastern
wall of the city, and carrying a bundle of lopped branches." Roman
soldiers assumed the forty-year-old father was a pagan. They seized
the weary worker and thrust him toward Jesus, who'd fallen for the
third time and seemed incapable of stumbling any farther.

"Simon was much annoyed," explained the nun, "and expressed
the greatest vexation at being obliged to walk with a man in so de-
plorable a condition of dirt and misery; but Jesus wept, and cast
such a mild and heavenly look upon him that he was touched, and
instead of continuing to show reluctance, [Simon] helped him to
rise, while the executioners fastened one arm of the cross on his
shoulders." As the procession continued, "Simon had not carried
the cross after Jesus any length of time before he felt his heart
deeply touched by grace."

The *Dolorous Passion* described Simon of Cyrene as a "stout-look-
ing man," and a fourth-century sarcophagus (stone coffin) from
Rome supports this description. The Passion Sarcophagus, probably
from the Catacomb of Domitilla, typifies an early Christian burial

The Passion Sarcophagus. Museo Pio Cristiano, the Vatican. Fourth century.

coffin; its sculpted front combines narrative and symbolism. In particular, this sarcophagus, now at the Vatican's Museo Pio Cristiano, depicts events leading to the Crucifixion. In the far-left panel, a short, chubby Simon resolutely carries the full cross with a Roman soldier stalking him.

To early Christians, Simon represented the need for every believer to daily bear the cross. Jesus had told his followers, "If anyone would come after me, he must deny himself and take up his cross daily and follow me. For whoever wants to save his life will lose it, but whoever loses his life for me will save it" (Lk 9:23-24).

Christians and Their Crosses

The image of a cross-bearing Simon on the Passion Sarcophagus might suggest how Christians envisioned themselves shouldering their own crosses. We'd expect Simon to hunch under the strain, clutching the cross with agony, his face grimaced and maybe resentful. Instead, he leans forward with legs slightly bent, like an athlete speed-walking toward a finish line. With formidable strength, Simon's left hand grips the cross while his right arm swings forward, keeping pace with his solid steps. His face looks childlike yet focused, undisturbed yet determined. He's not the expression of a man forced to work against his will.

Created a century after the Passion Sarcophagus, a relief sculpture in London's British Museum features Jesus carrying the cross and conveying a similar unharmed confidence. The Lord's left hand and shoulder balance the cross, while his right arm swings up to match his elongated strides. His serene face contrasts with a forward-moving body language. Jesus seems eager to attain his deathly destination.

Skipping another century, a Byzantine relief sculpture of the apostle Peter carrying his cross imitates the eager movements of Simon and Jesus. With his outer garment flying behind him, a somber Peter runs toward the enthroned Christ carved on the Apostles' Sarcophagus at the Sant' Apollinare in Classe church in Ravenna, Italy. In this sixth-century rendering, shouldering the cross appears incidental to reaching the resurrected Lord. In fact, Peter's fingers don't fully grasp the cross in his left hand, as if he'd discard it soon.

Several centuries later Christian artists began creating a suffering Christ carrying his cross up to Golgotha. But these early sarcophagi comforted mourners with the ultimate reward. As Christians willingly bore their own crosses, they could eagerly journey toward a heavenly destination. They could remember the apostle Paul's admonition:

> Therefore, since we are surrounded by such a great cloud of witnesses, let us throw off everything that hinders and the sin that so easily entangles, and let us run with perseverance the race marked out for us. *Let us fix our eyes on Jesus, the author and perfecter of our faith, who for the joy set before him endured the cross, scorning its shame, and sat down at the right hand of the throne of God.* Consider him who endured such opposition from sinful men, so that you will not grow weary and lose heart. (Heb 12:1-3, italics added)

Toward the end of the second century, an Athenian apologist echoed Paul's encouragement when he explained the eager hope of Christians. Athenagoras wrote, "We are persuaded that when we are removed from the present life we will live another life, better than the present one. It will be a heavenly life, not an earthly one. For we will abide near God, and with God, free from all change or suffering in the soul."

Paul and Athenagoras wrote these words for us, too. The crosses we bear today will fade and crumble in the light of heaven's glory.

6

The Garden and Golgotha

Then the Lord said to [Moses], "What is that in
your hand?""A staff," he replied. —EXODUS 4:2

The Shepherd's Cross

AN ANCIENT ISLAMIC STORY READS like an embellished version of
an Old Testament incident. With staff in hand, Moses challenges
the pharaoh in an Indiana Jones fashion, but the snake speaks up
and refers to Allah.

> Moses flung his staff upon the ground, and instantly it was
> changed into a serpent as huge as the largest camel. It glared at
> Pharaoh with fire-darting eyes, and lifted his throne to the ceil-
> ing. Openings its jaws, [the serpent] cried aloud, "If it pleased
> Allah, I could not only swallow up the throne with thee and all
> that are here present, but even thy palace and all that it contains,
> without any one perceiving the slightest change in me."

Copying the Jews and Christians before them, Muhammadans glo-
rified the supernatural powers of Moses' staff and praised God for it.

Judaic scholars believe Muslims derived their Moses anecdote from Jewish sources. In turn, rabbinical literature and the haggadah, a text for the Passover, wove "staff stories" throughout Jewish history, claiming the same rod assisted several revered Jewish leaders. For example, the *Midrash Yelamdenu,* a text of teachings, assigned a sacred lineage to this piece of wood, beginning with Jacob:

> The staff with which Jacob crossed the Jordan is identical with that which Judah gave to his daughter-in-law Tamar. It is likewise the holy rod with which Moses worked, with which Aaron performed wonders before Pharaoh, and with which, finally, David slew the giant Goliath. David left it to his descendents, and the Davidic kings used it as a scepter until the destruction of the Temple, when it miraculously disappeared. When the Messiah comes it will be given to him for a scepter in token of his authority over the heathen.

Beginning its story earlier than the midrash, the haggadah taught that God created the rod in the twilight of Creation's sixth day. Allegedly, several men, including the patriarchs, owned the staff before it passed to Judah. A later midrash also confused Moses' staff that worked miracles with Aaron's rod that budded, determining his tribe's priestly duties. Eventually, both the miraculous lineage and identity confusion merged into a Christian version of the staff's journey through biblical history, linking it to the wood of the cross.

The Christian Lineage

In the early thirteenth-century *The Book of the Bee,* a Syrian named Solomon expanded on the staff's lineage. He delineated a seamless Jewish and Christian heritage, mixing biblical and extra-biblical details into a curious legend, starting with the first couple. Although Solomon belonged to the Nestorian sect with its unorthodox views about Christ's divinity and humanity, his chapter "The

History of Moses' Rod" chronicles an intriguing, though implausible, succession.

According to the *Bee's* legend, the wood used for Christ's cross originated as a fragment of the Tree of Knowledge that tempted Adam and Eve and influenced their fall from grace. Adam used the wood as a staff. After Adam's death, his son Seth took the rod, used it as a weapon, and later gave it to Noah. Shem, a son of Noah, and the patriarchs Abraham, Isaac and Jacob each possessed the rod. Abraham destroyed his father's idols with the rod and carried it during his travels. Jacob fed his flocks with it.

Then the rod passed to Judah, the fourth of Jacob's twelve sons. Judah gave the rod to his daughter-in-law Tamar, disguised as a prostitute, as a pledge to send a goat to her after their sexual liaison. After Judah, the wood fragment descended to Pharez [Perez], an ancestor of King David and Jesus of Nazareth. When Pharez died, an angel carried the rod to Moab's mountains and buried it there. Later Jethro, the father-in-law of Moses, discovered it. Jethro offered the rod to Moses as a wedding gift. In Egypt, Moses performed miracles with it. He also carried the rod while leading the Israelites in their desert wanderings.

Moses passed the rod to Joshua, who used it to conquer and settle in the Promised Land. Joshua bequeathed the rod to Phineas, probably the grandson of Aaron, who buried it in Jerusalem. After the birth of Jesus, an angel revealed the rod's location to Joseph, the child's father. Joseph carried it with him on the journey into Egypt with Mary and Jesus. Joseph eventually gave the rod to James, the brother of Jesus. Judas Iscariot stole the rod from James. Before the crucifixion, Judas handed the rod to Christ's accusers. They transformed it into the transverse beam of the Lord's cross.

Vesting in the Power

This "genealogy of the wood" is a far-fetched story, but it underscores an early belief in the sacredness and power of Christ's cross. However, when early church leaders referred to "the power of the cross," they meant the power of God in Christ, who died on the cross.

The apostle Paul trusted this power when he wrote to Christians in Corinth. He explained, "For Christ did not send me to baptize, but to preach the gospel—not with words of human wisdom, lest the cross of Christ be emptied of its power. For the message of the cross is foolishness to those who are perishing, but to us who are being saved it is the power of God" (1 Cor 1:17-18). In the third century Origen, a Christian theologian, vested in symbolism about the rod, the cross and the true source of power. He believed the "rod of Moses, with which he subdued the Egyptians, is the symbol of the cross of Jesus, who conquered the world."

We can reflect on Origen's rod-and-cross symbolism with the stylized Shepherd's Cross, a lesser-known sign that combines a staff and a cross, memorializing Christ's roles as the Good Shepherd and the crucified Savior. The crook at the top of this cross also recalls the shepherd Moses, who freed his nation and foretold Christ's power to deliver humanity from sin. An ancient and rare example of the Shepherd's Cross remains on a marble stone in the ruins of St. John's Church in Turkey, built in Ephesus by Emperor Justinian during the sixth century. The crook slightly flares out, suggesting a twisting serpent and intensifying the symbolic reference to Moses and Christ.

Like the early Christians, the Shepherd's Cross affirms what God's power accomplished through Christ. First Peter 2:24 proclaims, "He himself bore our sins in his body on the tree, so that we might die to sin and live for righteousness; by his wounds you have been healed. For you were like sheep going astray, but now you have returned to the Shepherd and Overseer of your souls."

The Powerful Shepherd

The Shepherd's Cross expands my image of Jesus the Shepherd. As a

child I examined Sunday School illustrations of a serene Jesus, standing among the sheep and cradling a lamb in his arms. I resonated with
the psalmist who declared the Lord as his Shepherd, making him lie
down in green pastures, leading him beside quiet waters, and com-
forting him with a staff (Ps 23:2, 4). In my imagination, Jesus the
Shepherd was nurturing, soft-spoken and endlessly patient. I didn't
think of a shepherd as powerful. Yet when danger lurked, a shepherd
used the wood he carried to beat off attackers or pull wayward sheep
back from danger. He single-mindedly, even ferociously, searched until he found a lost sheep.

As an adult, I need this powerful Shepherd, the Lord who destroys
spiritual enemies and tracks me down when I stray. I want Christ the
Shepherd, the resurrected Saviour, to express his fierce love for me
and to protect me with his staff no matter the cost. This is the Good
Shepherd, the one who lays down his life for his sheep (Jn 10:11). I
want to depend on the lineage of this Shepherd, the one who leads us
to heaven and wipes away tears from our eyes (Rev 7:17).

Gentle yet strong. Sacrificial yet powerful. This is the Shepherd
who miraculously journeyed from Glory to Golgotha and back.

7

Inscription Insights

Pilate had a notice prepared and fastened to the cross.
It read: "Jesus of Nazareth, King of the Jews." —JOHN 19:19

The Proclamation Cross

Early in the morning a frustrated Pilate peered at the prisoner Jesus. "Are you the king of the Jews?" asked the Roman governor. "Yes," replied Jesus. "It is as you say."

Despite a flurry of accusations from the Jewish chief priests nearby, an incredulous Pilate couldn't pry more responses from Jesus. The silence sealed the prisoner's fate. Jesus would be crucified. This decision pleased the accusers. A true and righteous Jewish king wouldn't be condemned to crucifixion. Jesus couldn't really be king of the Jews.

But perhaps Pilate wasn't so sure.

Custom required posting a sign called a *titulus cruces* above the crucified person's head, listing his crimes. Pilate dictated the Lord's inscription as, "Jesus of Nazareth, the King of the Jews" (Jn 19:19). Disturbed by this identification, the chief priests confronted Pilate again. "Don't call him king of the Jews," they argued. "Say that he *claimed* to be king of the Jews."

Pilate refused. "What I have written, I have written," he answered (Jn 9:22).

The Audacious Inscription

With so many events to commemorate during a Passion week, the *titulus* nailed to Jesus' cross usually recedes compared to other grueling and glorious aspects of his crucifixion and resurrection. With the exception of John, the gospel books only briefly mention the *titulus*. However, by piecing together information from all the gospels we can assemble a better picture of this rough board that identified the suffering Jesus. The Matthew gospel notes that the superscription hung over Jesus' head (Mt 27:37). The Mark and Luke gospels say it was written, but their records of the wording differ (Mk 15:26; Lk 23:38). The John gospel reveals that Pilate dictated the title, written in three different languages (Jn 19:19-20). These languages include Aramaic for native Jews, Latin for Roman soldiers and Greek for visiting foreigners.

Still, these details don't expose the audacity of the inscription "King of the Jews" in the minds of first-century Jewish leaders. They believed Jesus disregarded their sacred past and blasphemed God.

Turning the pages of Jewish history, when judges ruled the land, ancient Israel was a tiny nation compared to its menacing enemies. Yet becoming Israel's king held no small consequence. God called these twelve tribes his chosen people. When Samuel the great judge retired, the Israelites didn't want to appoint another judge to govern their tribes. Instead, they demanded a king. The people wanted to resemble the nations around them, to fight their battles with a crowned ruler at the lead. This displeased God, but he granted their request and Samuel anointed Saul as the first king of Israel, the king of the Jews.

Although Saul failed as a ruler, the Jews revered certain past kings. They believed the sovereign God designated kings and their ruling descendents. Not just anyone—especially the radical Jewish nobody from Nazareth—could assume the same role as their King David. Later generations of Jews declared that David "destroyed the enemies on every side" and God "took away his sins, and exalted his horn for ever: he gave him a covenant of kings, and a throne of glory in Israel."

Coupled with this history, first-century Jews lived in captivity, under Roman rule. They couldn't declare a king. To Roman leaders, naming someone "King of the Jews" signaled setting up a rebel government, an uprising that Pilate would quickly crush. In reality, these Jews yearned for the Messiah, a spiritual savior instead of a crowned monarch. But Jesus didn't fulfill their expectations for a messiah, either. Hailing him as King of the Jews—even as a mocking irony—deeply offended their sacred sensibilities. Clearly, Pilate was sneering at them.

The Mysterious Fragment

Early Christians also turned their eyes toward the Savior's *titulus,* but in a twist of meaning, they honored its inscription. By the early Middle Ages believers easily recognized the initials *INRI* as an abbreviation for *Iesvs Nazarenvs Rex Ivdaeorvm.* Or "Jesus of Nazareth, the King of the Jews" in Latin. Eventually the inscription—and then the abbreviation—appeared in Western sculpture and paintings of the crucifixion.

For example, the British Museum in London owns a carved plaque from the fifth century, described as the "earliest known narrative portrayal of the crucifixion." Originally mounted to a square ivory casket (container), the small sculpture deftly articulates the inscription *REX IUD [AEORUM]* or "King of the Jews" above Christ's head. At the end of the Middle Ages and into the Renaissance the crucifixion paintings of artists like Pietro Cavallini, Andrea Mantega and Antonello da

Messina reduced the titulus inscription to *INRI*. Artists continue this practice today, and most Christians recognize the sign of the Proclamation Cross. It's a simple Latin cross, adorned only with the *INRI* letters on a titulus or banner.

While some artifacts from early Christianity display an INRI cross, the Church of Santa Croce in Rome claims ownership of a fragment of Christ's actual titulus. It's only a small piece with the inscription *"NAZARINUS R,"* or "Nazareth K(ing)" in Hebrew, Greek and Latin. It's never been scientifically tested, but one scholar states, "The evidence is teasing." The relic undoubtedly appears ancient, and aligns with the Roman practice of whitewashing the board for plainer readability. However, it's odd that the Greek and Latin inscriptions are backwards, in the style of Hebrew writing. Many scholars dismiss the relic, but it's never been declared authentic or forged.

Yet despite the hesitations of powerful governors and knowledgeable scholars, Christ's role didn't remain uncertain. Years later the apostle Paul explained to the church at Ephesus, "And [God] made known to us the mystery of his will according to his good pleasure, which he purposed in Christ, to be put into effect when the times will have reached their fulfillment—to bring all things in heaven and on earth together under one head, even Christ" (Eph 1:9-10).

The inscription was accurate. He is the King of the Jews.

He is King of us all.

The Man of Sorrows

*He was despised and rejected by men, a man of
sorrows, and familiar with suffering.* —ISAIAH 53:3

The Man of Sorrows

I HADN'T SUSPECTED THAT A MONTH-LONG business trip to Lithuania
would challenge my perception of Christ and his anticipation of the crucifixion. During my time off work, I often prowled through the streets
of Vilnius, the capital city, absorbing the nation's culture, history and
artwork. One weekend I also ventured into the countryside with a gra-
cious English-speaking family. Primeval forests populate a fourth of the
land, and as a result, it also abounds with wooden folk art.

Lithuania is the home of a ubiquitous woodcarving, the *Rupintojelis.*
This word translates as "anxiety, concern and solicitude." Artists carve
the wooden statue in many styles, but always it depicts a sitting man,
bent over with his elbow on his knee and head in his hand. Depending
on how an observer perceives the man's expression, he looks pensive,
worried or sorrowful. I couldn't ignore the *Rupintojelis.* He sat in
homes, beckoned from shop windows, weathered outdoor markets,

marked dirt crossroads, inhabited rustic shrines, and along with the plentiful amber, served as a popular souvenir for tourists.

Some scholars think the *Rupintojelis* appeared in Lithuania several centuries ago, as a way for villagers to express their own fears and worries. Eventually the carving evolved into the Man of Sorrows or Pensive Christ, a representation of Christ and his sorrow for the world, or his distress about the approaching crucifixion. Most of the wood sculptures I examined depicted a Christ who looked worried.

A worried Christ? This rattled my understanding of Scripture. I knew that as a man, Jesus expressed anger, sorrow and other emotions, but worry pushed me too far. I couldn't reconcile it with his participation in the Godhead. I couldn't imagine the holy and perfect Son of God worrying. I started to worry about the Jesus who looked worried.

Maybe this was just a matter of semantics and artistic style, because I accepted a troubled Christ in the Garden of Gethsemane (Mt 26:36-38). Whatever the case, as I encountered more of these carvings, I thought more about the man of sorrows described by the prophet Isaiah (Is 53:3). When I thought of Christ's suffering, I had limited it to the Passion Week. The *Rupintojelis* forced me to consider his other sorrows, the years before he approached the cross.

Sorrow in Scripture

Scripture mentions or alludes to some of the Lord's sorrows. When Mary and Joseph lost track of their young son, Jesus, they later found him conversing with teachers in the temple courts. Jesus reprimanded his mother and father by saying, "Why were you searching for me? . . . Didn't you know I had to be in my Father's house?" (Lk 2:49). Could his words have edged with sorrow for the parental lack of understanding? Might he have repressed a similar feeling when his mother fretted about wine at the wedding in Cana (Jn 2:4)? Did he feel sad or weary when the bleeding woman's touch sapped him of power (Lk 8:46)?

Jesus wept at the tomb of Lazarus (Jn 11:35). He mourned over Jerusalem and cried out, "O Jerusalem, Jerusalem, you who kill the prophets and stone those sent to you, how often I have longed to gather your children together, as a hen gathers her chicks under her wings, but you were not willing!" (Lk 13:34). He agonized in the Garden of Gethsemane, and implored, "My Father, if it is possible, may this cup be taken from me. Yet not as I will, but as you will" (Mt 26:39). He expressed distress when his disciples, for the third time, couldn't stay awake and pray with him (v. 45). We don't know how many times Jesus actually sorrowed, but when soldiers mounted Jesus on the cross, he was already familiar with grief. He was already a man of sorrows.

Even so, the sorrow continued. Looking down from the cross, Jesus painfully arranged for the separation from his mother, telling John the disciple, "Here is your mother" (Jn 19:27). Later he cried out, "'*Eloi, Eloi, lama sabachthani?*'—which means, 'My God, my God, why have you forsaken me?'" (Mt 27:46). He was the Savior in despair.

The Sorrow of the Cross

A continent away from Lithuania, flipping through a catalog of the Metropolitan Art Museum's exhibition *The Glory of Byzantium,* I'm struck again by the sorrowing Jesus. At first glance, a scarred panel called *The Man of Sorrows* looks like he still hangs on the cross. His neck no longer supports his head; it drops to his shoulder. His closed eyes and mouth can no longer express pain. With closer scrutiny, though, I notice the Lord's arms pressing against his sides instead of extending on a crossbeam. This is Christ's body without a spirit, growing cold during the interval between the Crucifixion and the Resurrection. The art commentator describes Christ as "erect, yet dead, in glory and yet utterly debased." In this death-stricken pose, a sign of the cross frames his head.

The catalog's *The Man of Sorrows* is the earliest known image with this title, painted in the twelfth century. Around the year eleven hundred Byzantines originated the image *Akra Tapeinosis,* the Utmost Humiliation. Later this image became the Man of Sorrows paintings of Western Christianity. The artists of Byzantium, the Eastern part of the Roman Empire, explored Christ's sorrowful nature. Perhaps unlike me, an insulated American, they intimately understood the ravages of war, the truth of a life cut off too early. They didn't shrink back from the decaying aftermath of Christ's death. Like their Savior, they touched sorrow.

Two thousand years after Christ's death on the cross, his sorrow also touches us. Professionals who work with the bereaved notice that people who've suffered can develop a remarkable depth of compassion. This is the suffering Jesus. The Man of Sorrows, acquainted with grief, understands our sorrows and grief. His rejection ministers to our rejection; his death walks with us through the physical and emotional deaths in our lives. He mourns our losses with us. The gospel writers repeatedly pointed out that when Jesus saw the multitudes, or when he met suffering individuals, he was filled with compassion. James 5:11 assures us, "The Lord is full of compassion and mercy." He knows we're vessels shaped from clay.

On the other hand, compassion already resided in the Son's nature before he descended to earth. He didn't need to die on the cross to acquire compassion. But Christ's familiarity with sorrow and suffering—as a human like us—can move us toward his compassion. Like us, he has suffered. Like us, he has mourned. The Man of Sorrows is also the God of all comfort.

9

Descent from the Cross

So Joseph [of Arimathea] bought some linen cloth,
took down the body, wrapped it in the linen, and
placed it in a tomb cut out of rock. —MARK 15:46

Descent from the Cross
in the **Codex Egberti**

JOSEPH OF ARIMATHEA MUST HAVE trembled. His dear friend Jesus
had just died, and he needed to ask Pilate for the body. Jews buried their
dead by sundown and the Sabbath approached, so he couldn't hesitate.

Joseph was endangering himself by asking for the remains of a sedi-
tious and crucified man, reviled by both Jews and Gentiles. Before
now he'd kept his belief in Jesus as the Son of God a secret. He was an
honored member of the Sanhedrin, the Jewish tribunal. But Joseph
couldn't leave Jesus hanging and stinking on that horrible cross—
paled, bloodied and wretched—for the scrutiny of mockers and gawk-
ers. Soldiers who ignored Jewish custom would ruthlessly tear down
the body, without grief or reverence, and toss it in a dump to suffer
further indignities by scavengers. Nobody should be treated that way,

and especially not his Lord.

Given this, Joseph mustered his courage and stood boldly before Pilate, the Roman prefect of Judea, the man with absolute authority over the Jews.

"Is Jesus already dead?" asked Pilate. Incredulous, he summoned the centurion who'd witnessed the crucifixion. When the official confirmed the teacher's death, Pilate bequeathed the body to Joseph (Mk 15:44-45).

Already prepared, Joseph headed to the crucifixion site with Nicodemus, another Jewish official no longer afraid to associate with Jesus. Joseph carried a swath of pure linen he'd carefully purchased before addressing Pilate. Nicodemus "brought a mixture of myrrh and aloes, about a hundred pound weight" (Jn 19:39). The men tenderly extracted the limp body and dressed it according to Jewish rituals. After placing Jesus on an anointing stone, they slathered on the spice mixture and wrapped him in linen strips. Securing the last piece of cloth, the two men reckoned with the inevitable. Their beloved teacher would soon lay in a tomb, locked away from their touch, their sight, their companionship.

Painting and Carving the Deposition

In the ninth century, paintings and sculpture of the *Apokathelosis,* the Deposition of Christ, became popular with Byzantine Christians. The tenderness of two prominent Jewish men taking down Christ's body resonated with the faithful, drawing them closer to their Savior's sacrifice. Perhaps their own memories of a loved one's death heightened the meaning and mourning inherent in this image. Certainly, the deposition had been sacred and life-changing.

One of the earliest Byzantine versions of the deposition helped to illustrate *The Homilies of Gregory of Nazianzus,* an illuminated manuscript of sermons often referred to as the Paris Gregory because it's cataloged in France's national library. Positioned on a multiple-image page between the Crucifixion and the Entombment, this miniature painting of the deposition is a simple arrangement. With Christ still hanging on the cross, Joseph and Nicodemus reach up to detach the body. Mary, the mother of Jesus, stands to the side, hands clasped in a Byzantine expression of grief.

During the tenth century, Western artists began depicting the same scene with the title *The Descent from the Cross.* An early example in the *Codex Egberti,* an illuminated manuscript created for the archbishop of Trier, Germany, illustrates both the "descent" and the entombment in one vertical frame. Figurally, the Ottonian composition is even simpler than the Paris Gregory, featuring only Joseph and Nicodemus with Jesus wrapped in a blue shroud. Joseph slings the limp body over his left shoulder while Nicodemus holds the legs. A cross stands behind the three figures, but not the Latin version of later paintings and sculpture. It's transformed into the Patriarchal or Archiepiscopal Cross with two crossbeams: a short beam at the top to represent the *titulus,* and a longer crossbeam for stretching out the arms. This cross signifies the authority of the soon-to-be risen Christ, acting as a harbinger of hope.

As the "Descent from the Cross" image flourished farther into the Middle Ages and beyond, the composition grew more complex. In the twelfth century the sculptor Benedetto Antelami carved the scene into the choir screen or pulpit in the cathedral at Parma, Italy. The sculpted marble figures divide into three groups. Lined up in single-file procession, mourners flank the left of the cross. A central group of Joseph and Nicodemus work at pulling down an oversized body of Jesus. A group to the right incorporates soldiers throwing dice for his robes, and male Jews, probably religious officials. Looking at this relief sculpture in a textbook, I'm compelled to touch the page, as if I might feel both the material and emotional texture of this moment.

Great artwork does that to me. It pulls me in closely, inviting me to participate and forcing me to think. Until I studied art history, I'd never asked, "What were the circumstances and mechanics of taking Christ down from the cross? Wasn't this an important prelude to Easter, too?"

When my mother died, the most poignant time unfolded soon after her spirit passed into eternity. I touched her face and hands, stroked her soft hair and helped apply cream to her still-warm body. I needed those last minutes to adore my mother, before strangers carted her away, before a well-meaning mortician turned her into "the deceased" I barely recognized.

Based on my experience, I can't help but think that for Joseph and Nicodemus, caring for the Lord's body constituted a final act of respect, but also a justification to tarry longer before the last goodbye. For me, the *Descent from the Cross* intertwines art imitating life and life imitating art. The *Descent from the Cross* recalls the sacredness of my mother's death. My mother's death echoes the holy transition in the *Descent from the Cross*. With this comparison, I recognize Christ's deposition to be as holy as any other Passion Week event. This is the power of sacred art.

This, too, is the surpassing power of God's Spirit. He accompanies us into the unwanted, the necessary, the ordinary, the unstoppable and the unspeakable to create hallowed and treasured moments.

PART THREE

Early Signs of Faith

The Cross and the First Believers

The cross was not a symbol of the earliest Christians, who preferred the anchor, the fish or Chi Rho. The crucifixion was a problem for the early Church, since it had to convince unbelievers of what would have seemed like a bizarre claim, that its God was a victim of this foul, and then still very current, form of punishment. Historically, crucifixion was not a punishment meted out by Jewish authorities, whose preferred method of execution was stoning: it was imported into Palestine by the Romans. . . . Therefore, it was a particular humiliation for Jesus the Jew to die on a Roman cross.

RICHARD TAYLOR,
HOW TO READ A CHURCH

10

Crucified with Christ

I have been crucified with Christ and I no longer live, but Christ lives in me. The life I live in the body, I live by faith in the Son of God, who loved me and gave himself for me. —GALATIANS 2:20

Saint Peter's Cross

T HE DAY JESUS COMMISSIONED HIS twelve disciples, he handed them a mixed bag of instructions. First he authorized the men of his inner circle to cast out evil spirits and "heal every disease and sickness" (Mt 10:1). But then the Master warned them: "I am sending you out like sheep into the midst of wolves; . . . they will hand you over to councils and flog you in their synagogues; and you will be dragged before governors and kings because of me, as a testimony to them and the Gentiles" (Mt 10:16-18 NRSV).

Jesus also told the disciples not to fear those "who kill the body," as if he expected murderers to plot against them (Mt 10:28). Spiritual power exacted a high personal price, and I wonder if a few disciples harbored second thoughts.

According to Christian tradition, the meeting recorded in Matthew only told part of the story. Of the twelve disciples, only John died a natural death. Depending upon the source consulted, up to six were crucified. When the apostle Paul wrote, "I have been crucified with Christ," the possibility of a literal crucifixion loomed nearby.

The Crucified Disciples

Evidently courage accompanied the disciples' spiritual power. After the Lord's death, most of them spread abroad to preach the gospel and eventually turned into martyrs honored by the church. It's impossible to confirm the exact facts of the disciples' deaths, and Christian groups vary according to what they believe. But most Christian traditions support that Peter, Andrew and perhaps Bartholomew died by crucifixion.

Peter served as a missionary to Asia Minor. When Emperor Nero waged his persecutions against Roman Christians, soldiers imprisoned, tortured and eventually killed this disciple. Peter felt unworthy to die in the same manner as Christ. So at his request, the executioners crucified him upside down. As a result, the inverted cross turned into a sign of humility, and it represents Peter in Christian symbolism.

One of the first disciples called by Jesus, Andrew served as a missionary to Achaia (southern Greece). Like Peter, Andrew asked to be crucified on a different cross than the Latin shape of Christ's crucifixion. As a result, he died on an X-shaped cross. Ancient Christians claimed he hung alive on this cross for two days, passionately preaching to his spectators. Andrew's "X" is a symbol of humility and martyrdom, and the official cross of Scotland.

Bartholomew (sometimes identified as Nathanael) preached the gospel in various countries, including Armenia and India. Some groups claim he was crucified upside-down after being flayed alive; others say he was beheaded. In Christian art he's usually depicted holding his own skin, as in Michelangelo's *Last Judgment* in the Vatican's Sistine Chapel.

It's been claimed that three other disciples died by crucifixion: Philip, Thaddeus (sometimes identified as Jude) and Simon. But whatever persecution and death threatened the original disciples, not one recanted his faith. Instead, early Christians reported attitudes like Andrew's. He saluted the cross and said, "I have long desired and expected this happy hour. The cross has been consecrated by the body of Christ hanging on it." It's hard to fathom this kind of happiness. Only someone fully assured of his faith and eternal destiny could utter such words.

The Assurance of Martyrs

"I am a Christian and we commit no wrongdoing," insisted Blandina, a young slave girl persecuted during the second century massacre of nineteen thousand Christians in the city of Lyons, Gaul (France). The frail Blandina endured so many afflictions she exhausted and baffled her torturers. A letter sent to Christians in Asia Minor described her ordeal: "Blandina was filled with such power as to be delivered and raised above those who were torturing her by turns from morning till evening in every manner, so that they acknowledged that they were conquered, and could do nothing more to her. And they were astonished by her endurance, as her entire body was mangled and broken and they testified that one of these forms of torture was sufficient to destroy life, not to speak of so many and so great sufferings." Still, Blandina claimed her faith and innocence.

After this, the tortures increased. Blandina was thrown to the wild beasts, speared with a gauntlet, roasted on an iron chair and suspended on a stake while exposed to wild beasts again. The report to Asia Minor claimed that from a distance, Blandina appeared "as if hanging on a cross." The beasts wouldn't touch the girl, and soldiers returned her to prison. As one of the last martyrs, Blandina finally was stuffed into a net, tossed by a wild steer and killed with a dagger. Persecutors burned her body and dumped its ashes into the Tiber River. The letter writer from Lyons emphasized, "The heathen themselves confessed that never among them had a woman endured so many and such terrible tortures."

Christian art usually depicts Blandina surrounded by beasts. Her charred body shaped into a cross and Peter's upside-down crucifixion uncomfortably expose the irony of Christ's death and resurrection. Faith in the meaning of Christ's cross ignites persecution, but the triumph of that same cross empowers us to endure it.

The early martyrs set a resounding example for Christians persecuted for their faith, expressed in Scripture by the apostle Paul:

> We are hard pressed on every side, but not crushed; perplexed, but not in despair; persecuted, but not abandoned; struck down, but not destroyed. We always carry around in our body the death of Jesus, so that the life of Jesus may also be revealed in our body. For we who are alive are always being given over to death for Jesus' sake, so that his life may be revealed in our mortal body. So then, death is at work in us, but life is at work in you. (2 Cor 4:8-12)

A Personal Comparison

Compared to the early Christian martyrs, my challenges seem small. I don't live in a country that demands a martyr's death for my faith. Even so, God wants to conform me to the image of Christ, and life continually serves up repeated opportunities to persevere, to be crucified with Christ, to put something within me to death so life can spring up. I can choose whether I'll engage the cross, humbly submit and die to myself. I need to forsake the sins and habits that strangle my soul, but too often I engage them without considering the consequences.

This is when the martyrs can exhort, inspire and sustain me. What is death, compared to the life to come? Just as physical death reaps eternal life, spiritual death harvests internal rewards. If I would submit, I might be less selfish and addicted, more humble and generous. I could live according to what frees rather than enslaves me.

Isaac Jogues, a Jesuit missionary and martyr from the seventeenth century, advised, "Whenever a man properly humbles himself grace gathers round." Lord, grant to me this humility so I can greet that grace.

11

The Everywhere Cross

*For God was pleased to have all his fullness dwell in him, and
through him to reconcile to himself all things, whether things on
earth or things in heaven, by making peace through his blood,
shed on the cross.* — COLOSSIANS 1:19-20

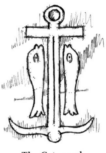

**The Catacomb
of Priscilla Anchor**

COMPARED TO OTHER PRACTICING religions of the first century,
Christianity bloomed late. Converted during the reign of Roman Emperor Tiberius, the first bands of Christians in the empire looked absurd pitted against the mythical figures staring at them from imperial
art and architecture. These gods, goddesses and super humans stood
on thousands of years of belief and worship, with hoards of their images reproduced in public and private venues, even on household objects. Christians worshiped a man crucified by the Romans, and had
nothing visually to show for it. As far as we know, Christian images
didn't appear until around AD 200, not even depictions of Jesus.

In the second century the Christian apologist Saint Clement of Alexandria emphasized worshiping God instead of representing him through art. He believed pictures of the divine degraded it, and he didn't want Christians to fall into idolatry like pagan worshipers. In fact, Clement ridiculed images of the gods and goddesses revered by Roman citizens. He called them idols manipulated by demons who mocked God.

Still, Clement was pragmatic. Christians in the Roman Empire needed signet rings for business transactions. However, the available intaglios (designs incised on the gems) often represented pagan religions. So Clement advised Christians to carefully select intaglios for their signet rings, using readymade gems and their seals. Certain symbols mirrored Christian stories and beliefs and believers could use them with good conscience. However, they were to avoid symbols contrary to their faith and morality.

Clement wrote specific advice, suggesting what images Christians could incise on their rings. He advised:

> Our seals should be a dove or a fish or a ship running in a fair wind or a musical lyre such as the one Polycrates used or a ship's anchor as the one Seleucus had engraved on his sealstone. And if someone is fishing he will call to mind the apostle [Peter] and the children drawn up out of the water [baptized]. We who are forbidden to attach ourselves to idols must not engrave the face of idols [on our rings], or the sword or the bow, since we follow the path of peace, or drinking cups, since we are sober. Many licentious people carry images of their lovers and favorite prostitutes on their rings.

Clement devised a plan to keep Christians in a spiritual and physical safety zone. The dove, fish, ship, harp and anchor already existed as decorative art in the Roman culture, but on the hands of Christians, they emanated different meanings. By using these images believers stamped their signatures without compromising their faith. Essentially, they kept the status quo and shopped in existing markets without raising the eyebrows of pagan vendors.

The Cross in the Culture

If early Christians followed Clement's advice and chose an anchor or a ship for their signet rings, they sealed their business with a sign of the cross. But even before Clement's ring concerns, early believers often interpreted the anchor with its crossbar and a ship with its mast as Christ's cross (although both of these images carry other meanings). Scholars classify everyday images that represented the cross as "crypto-crosses." Accordingly, archaeologists have found gems inscribed with anchors and ships, consistent with Clement's suggestion and era.

Anchor and ship images also decorate Rome's catacombs that pre-date Constantine's reign, and sometimes the anchors appear with fish, a common sign for Christ's followers. For example, two fish frame the shank of an anchor on a titulus (inscription in stone) in the Catabomb of Priscilla (see illustration on p. 68). In the Catacomb of Domitilla, a fish appears to be attached to each fluke (spade-shaped part) of another anchor etched in stone. Both anchor-fish images represent the Christian's close association with the cross.

If the anchor and the ship mast seem like stretching symbolism too far, literature from early church leaders supports identifying Christ's cross in the natural world. Minucius Felix, one of the first apologists, refuted rumors that Christians worshiped crosses, but he still saw their images everywhere. "And, surely, your military ensigns, standards and banners, what are they but gilded and decorated crosses?" he asked. "Your trophies of victory copy not merely the appearance of a simple cross but that of a man fastened to it as well. And as for the sign of the cross, there is no doubt that we see it in the world of nature around us: when you see a ship gliding with oars extended."

The second-century apologist Justin Martyr also saw the cross in everyday life and in the human form. He wrote:

> For consider all the things in the world, whether without this form they could be administered or have any community. For the sea is not traversed except that trophy which is called a sail abide safe in the ship; and the earth is not ploughed without it: diggers and mechanics do not their work, except with tools which have this shape. And the human form differs from that of the irrational animals in nothing else than in its being erect and having the hands extended, and having on the face extending from the forehead what is called the nose, through which there is respiration for the living creature; and this shows no other form than that of the cross.

At a time when Christians couldn't display their faith openly, they saw the cross all around them. Deprivation enhanced their senses, creativity and appreciation for its meaning. In contrast, our "cross senses" have dulled. When we walk past a cross attached to a church, what do we think? If we spot a street sign for an intersection, in the shape of a cross, do we ponder Christ's sacrifice? Snapping the clasp on a cross medallion, do we cherish the ornament's meaning? These moments, these recognitions, could be as devotional as the daily pages we read or the rituals we keep.

12

Graffiti Marks and Mocks

*But we preach Christ crucified: a stumbling blockto Jews and foolishness
to Gentiles, but to thosewhom God has called, both Jews and Greeks, Christ
the power of God and the wisdom of God.* —1 CORINTHIANS 1:23-24

The Palatine Hill Graffiti

ONE OF THE EARLIEST FORMS OF Christian art isn't a painting, sculpture or even a catacomb fresco. It's a patch of graffiti on plaster, discovered in the *Pædagogium* on the Palatine Hill in Rome and dated to around 200 AD. Imperial teachers used the *Pædagogium* building to educate the emperor's staff, and perhaps an idle student etched the crude artwork. The drawing depicts a man with an ass's head, hanging on a cross. Viewed from behind, the crucified man turns to the left, looking down at a youth with a raised arm. An inscription underneath the cross figure claims in Greek, "Alexamenos worships his god."

Art historians disagree whether the scrawled words should be interpreted as a Christian's profession of faith or a pagan's scorn. On the one hand, Jesus rode into Jerusalem on an ass, so it became an important symbol for early Christians. From this perspective, some scholars suggest drawing the crucified Christ with a donkey's head paid homage to a hailed Savior. On the other hand, most observers recognize the inscription as a taunt from someone who misunderstood the new religion. During this era a rumor circulated through Rome that Christians worshiped the head of an ass.

In the second century the pagan Marcus Cornelius Fronto, an orator and the tutor of Emperor Marcus Aurelius, reported, "I hear that they adore the head of an ass, that basest of creatures, consecrated by I know not what silly persuasion. . . . [He] who explains their ceremonies by reference to a man punished by extreme suffering for his wickedness, and to the deadly wood of the cross, appropriates fitting altars for reprobate and wicked men, that they may worship what they deserve."

Fronto ridiculed a sacred focal point of the nascent faith: Christ's cross. To pagans the cross represented humiliation heaped on criminals, and anyone who worshiped a man hanging on this torture-and-death device deserved to be mocked. Why would anyone adore defeat?

Mocking the Cross

Although cross mockery might be disturbing, it shouldn't be surprising. As Christ approached his death, both Jews and Gentiles mocked his agonizing cross journey. Before his triumphal entry into Jerusalem, he told the disciples, "the Son of Man will be betrayed to the chief priests and the teachers of the law. They will condemn him to death and will turn him over to the Gentiles to be mocked and flogged and crucified" (Mt 20:18-19). The mob that demanded Christ's death hurled insults at him. After Pilate ordered Christ's flogging, the governor's soldiers dressed him in purple, smashed a crown of thorns on his head and mocked their captive as "King of the Jews." The crowd ridiculed Christ as he bent under the wood beam's weight, stumbling toward Golgotha. The chief priests, elders, guards and bystanders

heckled Christ as he hung on the cross in unconscionable pain. Even a
robber crucified next to Christ scorned him.

In effect, Christ's crucifixion initiated an enduring propensity to
mock the cross. Pagan scholars, satirists and philosophers announced
its absurdity. Lucian, a satirist and novelist from the second century,
commented about Christians, "You know, they worship that great
man of theirs, who was put on a gibbet in Palestine, because he added
this new mystery to human life." Lucian delivered his crucifixion quip
as a side comment, but other opponents of Christianity penned
straightforward mockery.

Toward the end of the second century, the Greek philosopher Cel-
sus wrote a book to refute the Christians. In *True Doctrine*, he poked
fun at the instrument of Christ's death. He claimed:

> Everywhere they speak in their writings of the tree of life and
> of resurrection of the flesh by the tree—I imagine because
> their master was nailed to a cross and was a carpenter by trade.
> So that if he had happened to be thrown off a cliff, or pushed
> into a pit, or suffocated by strangling, of if he had been a cob-
> bler or a stonemason or blacksmith, there would have been a
> cliff of life above the heavens, or a pit of resurrection, or a rope
> of immortality, or a blessed stone, or an iron of love, or the
> holy hide of leather.

Against the Christians

The great intellectual Porphyry wrote a fifteen-volume treatise,
Against the Christians, at the end of the third century. Only fragments
of the work remain, but it's evident that Porphyry considered the
crucifixion preposterous and Christ's behavior embarrassing. He
wrote, "But even if Christ had to suffer according to God's com-
mands, and was obliged to endure punishment, yet at least he should
have endured his passion with some boldness, and uttered words of

force and wisdom to Pilate his judge, instead of being mocked like any gutter-snipe."

Ironically, pagan criticism probably solidified Christian behavior and doctrine sooner than if believers had merely conversed among themselves. Although most Christians emerged from the lower classes and avoided battles about their beliefs, some well-educated believers responded with defenses of the faith. Early church fathers and others left behind documents that defended Christianity to pagans and guided believers in their thinking. When pagans delivered blistering attacks, many professing Christians defected back to paganism. Yet others held firm, fortified by their faith, communities and a maturing, written belief system. About the cross, Ignatius of the first century wrote, "For me the documents are Jesus Christ; my unassailable documents are his cross, and his death and resurrection, and the faith that is through him." Christ's death on the cross remained the heart of Christian redemption.

Giving a Defense

Of course, mocking the cross didn't end when paganism declined, along with the Roman Empire, in the late fifth century. Despising the cross festered through the ages and still exists today. So should contemporary Christians defend the mockery? I'm not sure a clear-cut answer exists.

When Christ's critics mocked him, Scripture says he didn't answer (Mt 26:63), although he had stated his opinions to accusers before then. In contrast, early church fathers felt compelled to defend their beliefs, strengthening the faith of Christians, and in some cases, saving them from persecution. Some apologists even mocked the pagans in return. In between, the author of 1 Peter suggested how Christians should defend themselves: "Always be prepared to give an answer to everyone who asks you to give the reason for the hope that you have. But do this with gentleness and respect" (1 Pet 3:15).

However we decide to respond to mockers, there's one thing to remember. Despite our desire for acceptance or being "right," the cross will always spark dissension. Before Christ's return, there will never be a time when everyone believes.

13

The Sign of Jonah

For as Jonah was a sign to the Ninevites, so also will
the Son of Man be to this generation. —LUKE 11:30

Catacombs of Saint Callixtus

THE PAINTING LOOKS LIKE A Saturday-morning cartoon from the
early days of television. A small boat shaped like a melon slice rocks in
a transparent sea, with three almost-naked men perilously on deck.
One man clings to the ship's unstable mast; another throws up his
hands in desperation. The third man, about to fall into the water,
looks like a sloppy diver with arms and legs flailing. A few feet away,
a daffy dragon-like creature pokes his head above the water, eager for
his soon-to-plunge meal.

It's the story of Jonah and the big fish, sponsored by the Old Testament and the Catacombs of Saint Callixtus during third-century Rome.

Descending into the underground burial sites for Christians, it's
striking to find that fresco (wall painting) scenes from the Old Testament dominate over those from the apostolic documents that later

composed the New Testament. Tourists might expect that paintings from Christ's life would flourish, but in Christian art dating up to the fourth century, themes from the Hebrew Scriptures appear four times more than New Testament images.

Jonah fresco. The catacombs of Saint Callixtus. Third century.

The story of Jonah wins as the favored Old Testament subject, with almost one-hundred depictions of him painted in the catacombs and sculpted on sarcophagi during the era before Emperor Constantine. The images divide the runaway prophet's story into three parts: the big fish swallows him up; the fish vomits him out; he despondently sits under a gourd vine. Although surviving Christian sculpture before Constantine is rare, one of the few sets of marble figures, now in the Cleveland Museum of Art, also tells the Jonah story. Distant runner-ups in the catacombs include Noah in the ark, Moses striking the rock, Abraham offering up Isaac, Adam and Eve and Daniel in the lion's den. From the New Testament, only the baptism of Jesus and the raising of Lazarus seem comparatively popular.

These strong Jewish roots make sense. The first Christians were Jews. They naturally identified with the Torah's narratives and considered Hebrew Scripture their heritage. They believed Jesus was the fulfillment of ancient prophecies about a coming Messiah, with word-of-mouth narratives and the apostles' instructions a continuation of God's spiritual intentions for them. First-century Christians kept the Hebrew laws and worshiped in synagogues and the Temple. Decades passed before Christianity grew distinct from Judaism, after the destruction of Jerusalem in AD 70.

Remembering the Old Testament

Even after this break from Judaism, Christians still retained their connection to Old Testament stories and teachings. Though their new theology freed them from the Law's rules (Rom 8:1-3), they revered the Torah's contribution and eventually included it in the canonical books of the Bible. Christians held to the Old Testament, along with the more recent writings of the apostles. They believed certain Jewish stories were typologies, serving as metaphors or "types" that foreshadowed Christ, the church or Christian sacraments.

The study of typology began with the teachings of Philo of Alexandria, a contemporary of the apostle Paul in the first century, followed by the third-century teacher Origen, also from Alexandria. Origen taught three levels of scriptural interpretation. First, we study the literal or historical meaning known through human senses. Second, we grasp the moral or typological meaning that touches the soul. Third, we ponder the allegorical or transcendent meaning that reaches the spirit.

This belief in multiple meanings coincided with the popular Old Testament and sometimes *Apocryphal* narratives that appeared in Christian art before the fourth century. In particular, the stories of Jonah, Noah, Moses, Abraham and Daniel relied on a redemptive message, as did less-popular images such as Susanna or Daniel and his friends in the furnace. So did New Testament stories like Jesus raising Lazarus from the dead. It's commonly surmised that Christians chose these narratives for the catacomb walls because they lived in an uncertain world, at times fraught with persecution. The most frequent images emphasized God's ability to deliver his spiritual children from peril, while on earth or by transporting them to heaven.

Overall, the popular redemptive images seemed to contribute to a whole theme, rather than appearing as isolated scenes. After the Emperor Constantine's rise to power, these deliverance and safety images diminished and Christian mourners selected more New Testament narratives. This probably happened because Christians no longer lived in peril, and more believers were Gentiles instead of converted Jews.

The catacomb depiction of Jonah's story may look primitive compared to our visual renditions, but the core message trumped the simple images. The prophet's ocean journey reminded early Christians of God's ability to rescue them. Even more, from a specific typology standpoint, the prophet pointed to Christ's bloody crucifixion and sealed-tomb resurrection. The ship's almost-obscured mast symbolized the Savior's cross. When Jonah splashed into the sea and the fish swallowed him, this foretold the Lord's death and burial. When the fish belched Jonah onto dry land, this represented the resurrection. The three days and nights in between patterned Christ's time in the sepulchre. Lest we think eager Christians conjured up this comparison, Christ told his cynics, "For as Jonah was three days and three nights in the belly of a huge fish, so the Son of Man will be three days and three nights in the heart of the earth" (Lk 12:40).

The keepers of the Catacombs of Saint Callixtus explain the comparison this way:

> The prophet Jonah, a biblical figure very dear to the early Christians, appears in all these cubicles. Jonah had preached repentance and conversion to the inhabitants of Nineveh, that is to the pagans. Jonah symbolizes the call to salvation of all men, whether Jews or pagans. Indeed, since the faithful buried in this crypt were originally all pagans, the prophet came to be the image of God's universal mercy. Jonah is also a symbol of resurrection.

The Joyful Resurrection

Recently I flipped through an icon catalog given to me by an Orthodox friend. I paused at a Jonah image from Meteora, Greece. The fish resembled a gigantic reptile with tiny fins and Jonah popped out of its mouth—hair, beard and robes unfazed—with an unrolling scroll in his left hand. Contrasted with the somber prophet portraits displayed on the page with Jonah, this painting looked whimsical. I laughed, but felt slightly irreverent among the somber faces of Byzantium. But isn't light-heartedness the point? Shouldn't the story's end turn jubilant?

In all my years as a Protestant, I've never woven Jonah into the Easter celebration. Perhaps I'm not observant, but I haven't seen his image incorporated into the Passion Week. (However, my Orthodox friend says his story figures into her church's observances.) Maybe in our corporate or personal worship we could learn from the Orthodox artist, creating a whimsical image or two of Jonah for our services or devotional times. Then we could laugh aloud that Christ has risen.

After an Easter Sunday service, in a burst of enthusiasm my friend Beth moved close to me and exclaimed, "Christ has risen!" She startled me, but then I thought, *Why shouldn't she feel joyful?*

He is risen indeed.

14

The Outstretched Hands

I lift up my hands toward your Most Holy Place. —PSALM 28:2

The *Donna Velata*

In the Roman Empire, Christians weren't the first to practice religious piety and prayer.

After Julius Caesar died in the first century BC, the empire posthumously deified him as a god. This meant his heir to the throne was the son of a god. It then became important for successive emperors to prove they descended from Caesar, even if through adoption. With this ancestry, emperors presented themselves as divine, but also humanly pious in their religious worship and practices.

Sometimes emperors compared themselves to mythical figures as another way to express their extraordinary natures and reinforce their right to divine rule. The Roman *Gemma Augustea,* a large onyx cameo from the first century AD, features the *apotheosis* (transformation into a god) of Emperor Augustus, with the ruler assuming the identity of Jupiter. The base of the Column of Antonius Pius, erected in Rome, depicts the second-century emperor and his wife Faustina on the wings of a male god, rising toward the sky in another *apotheosis*. A portrait bust of the mentally unstable Commodus, another second-century emperor, ridiculously depicts him as Hercules, with the head and skin of a lion perched on his head.

Roman citizens needed to please their god-emperors, but also the many other gods and goddesses of paganism. They revered and appeased these gods so hopefully their empire, and thus their lives, would be safe and prosperous. This required conducting the correct rituals to the appropriate gods for a mountain of needs, both in public ceremonies and private rituals. In the first book of Varro's *Antiquities*, the author explained that Romans venerated the gods to gain advantages from them. But to do this, worshipers needed a scrupulous understanding of a phonebook list of gods and their mythical abilities. They must understand "which god to invoke and for what purpose, in order not to be like those buffoons who ask Liber for water and the Nymphs for wine."

With the emphasis on religious appeasement, pagans spent significant time offering prayers and burning animal sacrifices to the gods. If certain gods weren't happy, then tragedies like famine, sickness or war might strike. If specific gods weren't appeased, nobody would get their daily needs met. Romans lived and worshiped in a perpetual state of religious anxiety about how to pray and keep rituals. They varied their prayer postures along with the sacrifices, but one intercessory stance became memorable because of its connection to Rome's catacombs.

The Posture of Prayer

On the outskirts of Rome, pagans, Jews and early Christians carved recesses deep in the soft tufa rock. From the third to fifth centuries, survivors often painted these catacomb walls with images that represented the deceased, and images of a person in prayer, the orans, appear in several catacombs. The *orans* (Latin for "praying") was a popular figure of late antiquity, usually depicted as a standing, veiled woman with her hands outstretched and gazing toward heaven. It's not always clear, however, whether an *orans* figure represented a pagan, Jewish or Christian worshiper. Each religious group used this stance as a prayer posture.

When an *orans* lifted up her hands in prayer, she expressed *pietas,* "the affectionate respect due to the state, to ruler, to family or to God." The *orans* appeared on the obverse side of Roman coins in the second and third centuries, with the appeal for a "righteousness that exalts a nation." Often a small stork representing family piety or a flaming altar accompanied the figure. In funeral contexts, the *orans* could have represented the deceased person's pious devotion in life or the soul's gratitude in paradise. In the pagan vernacular, the soul was feminine.

Probably the most famous painted *orans* from early Christianity stands on a wall in the Catacomb of Priscilla in Rome (see illustration p. 82). The third-century fresco dramatically exemplifies urgent prayer. The imploring eyes and enlarged hands, both lifted upward, beg God for deliverance. This *Donna Velata* (Veiled Lady) captures the submission and confidence of intercession.

Yet long before pagans in late antiquity lifted their hands in prayer, other civilizations used the same posture. In 1955 at the site of ancient Hazor in Galilee, archaeologists discovered a stone monument with two hands lifted to the sun. The hands represented the religious devotion of the Canaanites, around 1400 BC.

Old Testament Jews also lifted up their hands in prayer. From the desert of Judah, David prayed, "I will praise you as long as I live, / and in your name I will lift up my hands" (Ps 63:4). When King Solomon dedicated the temple, he "spread out his hands toward heaven" (1 Kings 8:22). A sorrowing nation of Israel declared, "Let us lift up our hearts and our hands / to God in heaven, and say: / 'We have sinned and rebelled / and you have not forgiven'" (Lam 3:41-42). Lifted hands praised, pleaded, lamented and repented to God, humbly acknowledging his holy authority.

Because early Christians were Jewish, they naturally lifted their hands in prayer, like the veiled *orans* figures in the catacombs. The apostle Paul advised the earliest Christians, "I want men everywhere to lift up holy hands in prayer, without anger or disputing" (1 Tim 2:8) and early church literature indicates the widespread practice of this prayer position. In the first through third centuries, Marcus Minucius Felix, Clement of Rome, Clement of Alexandria and Tertullian either advised Christians to lift up hands in prayer, or at least mentioned the practice. The distinguishing difference, however, was that Christians saw in the *orans* figure the outline of the cross. Standing up with arms and hands outstretched, she reminded them of their Lord's crucifixion. Her arms mimicked the transverse beam of Christ's torture.

Marcus Minucius Felix explained, "We assuredly see the sign of the cross . . . when a man adores God with a pure mind, with hands outstretched." Tertullian likened this prayer stance to Christ on the cross. "We, however, not only raise [our hands], but even expand them. Taking our model from the Lord's passion, even in prayer we confess to Christ," he wrote. But Tertullian didn't limit the cross to Christ's agony. In an earlier, chilling complaint, he'd acknowledged the suffering of Christians at the hands of persecutors. "With our hands thus stretched out and up to God, you tear us apart with your iron claws and hang us up on crosses," he declared. "The very posture of a Christian praying is one of preparation for all punishment."

Our World-Ravaged Hands

I think of the *orans* during the Eucharist, when the celebrant reads from The Book of Common Prayer: "He stretched out his arms upon the cross, and offered himself, in obedience to your will, a perfect sacrifice for the whole world." Some scholars think it's far-fetched to imagine the *orans* as the cross. But for me, the metaphor works. After all, Christ's death on the cross enables us to approach God. We can stretch out our world-ravaged hands to pray. We can cling to the cross.

Alone at home after the church service, I think about my own prayer stance. I'm too reserved. It's hard for me to pray with abandon like the *orans,* like Christ's posture on the cross. A lot of days it's difficult to pray at all. Yet something within me stirs. I glance at the closed door to my bedroom, and then risk it. I stretch out my arms and pray.

15

Signs of the Cross

Then he said to them all: "If anyone would come after me, he must deny himself and take up his cross daily and follow me." —LUKE 9:23

A Sign of the Cross

Cʜʀɪsᴛɪᴀɴ ᴛʀᴀᴅɪᴛɪᴏɴ ᴄʟᴀɪᴍs when Saint Anthony of Egypt retired to the remotest desert, devils tormented him in many frightening forms. But this fourth-century Christian, the earliest-known monastic, laughed at their impotence. When the dark side called, Anthony lifted his hand and symbolically traced the sign of the cross. He explained to his disciples, "Believe me, Satan fears the vigils, the prayers and the fasts of the devout; yea, one sign of the cross weakens him and puts him to flight."

Artwork and patristic literature affirm the early Christians' respect for this hand motion that outlined the shape of Christ's cross in the air or on their bodies. Depending on the era and location, believers made the sign of the cross to pray, express devotion, claim protection, bestow blessings, grant absolution, fight evil, practice sacred rituals and evoke Christ's presence and assistance throughout the day. Some sources believe Jesus taught this sign to his apostles, using it to bless them before his ascension to heaven. Others say John the Evangelist "signed himself" before dying, and the apostle Paul used it to restore a blind man's sight.

It's not possible to confirm the earliest, extra-biblical stories, but later church fathers commented on the sign of the cross in their writings. In the first century Ignatius, a disciple of the apostle John, wrote, "The sign of the cross is the trophy raised against the power of the prince of this world: When he sees it, he is afraid; when he even hears of it, he is filled with terror." Tertullian referred to the late second-century use of the sign. He explained, "At every forward step and movement, at every going in and out, when we put on our clothes and shoes, when we bathe, when we sit at the table, when we light the lamps, when on the couch, on a seat, and in all the ordinary actions of life, we trace the sign of the cross on our foreheads."

Later, during the fourth century, Bishop Cyril of Jerusalem remarked in his catechism, "Let us then not be ashamed to confess the Crucified. Be the cross our seal, made with boldness by our fingers on our brow and in every thing; over the bread we eat and the cups we drink, in our comings and in going; before our sleep, when we lie down and when we awake; and when we are at rest."

It's generally accepted that until the fourth century, Christians traced a small sign of the cross on their foreheads. Either boasting or lamenting Tertullian attested, "We Christians wear out our foreheads with the sign of the cross." However, Tertullian also revealed the practice of "signing" the cross on objects, like the woman who made the sign of the cross on her bed before retiring at night. By the fourth century the small sign extended to several parts of the body, but about two centuries later it transformed into just one, four-point movement traced across the chest or in the air.

Taking Up the Cross

Across the centuries Christians eventually differed in their approach to tracing the sign of Christ's cross. The tradition began by signing the forehead with a thumb. Western Christianity evolved into using an open hand, tracing the horizontal bar of the cross from left to right. The five open fingers represented the wounds of Christ. Eastern Christians brought the thumb, index finger and middle finger to a point, symbolizing the Trinity. The two remaining fingers pressed against the palm, representing Christ's human and divine natures. After tracing the two vertical points of the cross, they reversed the horizontal movement, from right to left.

In the twelfth century Pope Innocent III delineated the two methods for moving the hand between the shoulders. His instructions bordered on the poetic: "This is how it is done: from above to below, and from the right to the left, because Christ descended from the heavens to the earth, and from the Jews (right) to the Gentiles (left)" he explained. "Others, however, make the sign of the cross from the left to the right, because from misery (left) we must cross over to glory (right), just as Christ crossed over from death to life, and from Hades to Paradise."

In contrast to the open hand and three-fingered approach, some Orthodox Christians brought only the thumb and index fingers together. By the seventeenth century, a disagreement about whether to bring two or three fingers together contributed to a rift in the Russian Orthodox church. In the wake of the Reformation, signing oneself represented a meaningless ritual to new Protestants, and today nonliturgical Christians rarely use the sign, if at all.

Perhaps the gap between the "signers" and the "nonsigners" indicates how far we've traveled from this tradition's original meaning. Early Christians "signed themselves" to keep Christ foremost in their lives. Spiritually, they believed his power delivered them from eternal death and infused them with the strength to endure life. Yes, signing the cross can grow mechanical, reducing it to a thoughtless habit. But signing can also comfort, bolster and renew our sacred commitment. It can recall Christ's sacrifice. It can inspire us to take up our own cross daily and follow him.

16

The Absent Crucifixion

Surely he hath borne our griefs, and carried our sorrows:
yet we did esteem him stricken, smitten of God, and afflicted.
But he was wounded for our transgressions, he was bruised for
our iniquities:the chastisement of our peace was upon him;
and with his stripes we are healed. —ISAIAH 53:4-5 KJV

The Santa Sabina Crucifixion

IN EARLY FIFTH-CENTURY ROME, wooden church doors hardly constituted a novelty. But the great carved doors of the new Santa Sabina basilica, probably commissioned by Pope Celestine I, represented a significant spiritual shift. Based on the eighteen surviving relief sculptures, the original cypress doors divided into twenty-eight storytelling panels that visually presented episodes from the Old Testament and Christ's life. That's enough to merit the church's fame, but art historians note an unexplained breakthrough. The first panel, in the upper left of the door, illustrates the crucifixion. Two men flank an oversized Christ, all with their arms spread just below

shoulder height, but without visible crosses. Although some scholars
think the panel portrays the three Hebrews in a fiery furnace, most
agree it's among the first depictions of the crucifixion from late
antiquity.

Although Christ's message and redemptive acts depended on his
death and resurrection, for the most part, crucifixes didn't emerge
until the fifth century, and they rarely appeared until the seventh century. It's remarkable that early sacred art avoided the crucifixion, especially when the apostle Paul taught "Christ crucified" as the way to
salvation, and the ancient Eucharist liturgy celebrated Christ's death
and resurrection. Yet despite these emphases, artists avoided visual
representations of Christ nailed to the cross.

Theories and the Absent Cross

A few scholars have theorized about this absence. Art historian Nigel Spivey wonders if early Christians avoided artistic renditions of
Christ's suffering because of its atrocity. "Crucifixion was a punishment with a truly awful reputation in the Roman world," he explains. "It was death deserved by the most unworthy of unworthies;
it was death with grim humiliation, ignominy, and abasement. . . .
Who on earth would want its souvenir or remembrance?" It's possible that the scandalous crucifixion hit painfully "too close to
home." Consequently, Christians depicted the crucifixion metaphorically through images like the Lamb of God to lessen its grue-
someness. Perhaps they preferred focusing on hope instead of horror, deliverance rather than death.

Another theory about the crucifixion's absence speculates that
Christ' death was too great a mystery to recreate in image form. "The
issue is not only whether one can represent the incarnate deity visually, but also how one does it respectfully and truthfully, without pro-
faning a sacred mystery in finite material," notes another art historian,
Robin Margaret Jensen. Christians didn't want to appear as if they

practiced idolatry, elevating a man and his cross in a fashion similar to pagan worship.

Jensen also addresses a third, more common theory: "[It] has to do with public relations, propriety, and even safety as much as idolatry. Christians had reason to fear scorn and misunderstanding of their neighbors, especially in the era before the Peace of the Church [when Christians could worship freely]." Still, images of the crucifixion only tentatively appeared a century after Constantine allowed Christians to worship freely and banned this severe punishment. Even then, the images emphasized the Savior's triumph rather than his humiliation.

Many early Eastern images of the crucifixion revealed Christ as transformed and triumphant on the cross. For example, the sixth-century Rabbula Gospels contain one of the earliest illustrations of the crucifixion that includes many accurate biblical details, except Christ wears a long purple robe with two gold bands, the garb of royalty. During the early Middle Ages, depictions of Christ on the cross showed him alive instead of dead, placid instead of tortured. Centuries elapsed before images of a suffering Christ on the cross appeared.

Facing the Cruel Facts

Once the early Christian culture visually accepted the crucifixion and its pain, a more truthful image decorated the later Middle Ages. Toward the end of the tenth century, Gero, the archbishop of Cologne, commissioned a crucifix for his cathedral that demanded attention to the reality of Christ's death. Over six feet tall, the painted wood sculpture features a lifeless Christ still hanging on the cross. Christ's skin sags from holding the body's weight and his stomach bulges. His head hangs down, with the cratered eyes and contorted lips of prolonged suffering. "Not a symbolic sacrificial lamb of God, not a Byzantine emperor alive and crowned in front of a cross, not even a young hero, as in some Early Christian or Carolingian images, but a tortured martyr hangs in front of the worshiper," explains the art historian

Marilyn Stokstad. Everything about this sculpture cries, "It is finished." Christ has suffered. He is dead.

Although we know the cruel facts of Christ's death, the finality of the Gero cross and other realistic crucifixion images can challenge us. The excruciating pain beckons, asking us to consider his unconscionable sacrifice. We'd like to hurry past, and often we do. We keep the crucifixion absent from our minds. In fact, we like to exalt the empty cross; that Christ now lives and reigns in heaven. But looking squarely at the crucifixion can lead us to God's love. Ephesians 5:1-2 states, "Christ loved us and gave himself as a fragrant offering and sacrifice to God." When we reckon with the depth of Christ's sacrifice, we can accept the breadth of his love. We can begin to identify this love at work in us, in our world.

In our culture images of the cross appear so frequently, we barely notice. At the same time, we often don't sense God's love, forgiveness or presence. Could our cross-consciousness and our spiritual perceptions be cause and effect? We might not recognize God's gifts because we've ignored the cross. Who of us will contemplate Christ's cross long enough to find out?

PART FOUR

The Great Conversion

The Cross and Early Religious Freedom

We believe in one Lord, Jesus Christ, the only Son of God. . . . For us and for our salvation he came down from heaven: by the power of the Holy Spirit he became incarnate from the Virgin Mary, and was made man. For our sake he was crucified under Pontius Pilate; he suffered death and was buried. On the third day he rose again in accordance with the Scriptures; he ascended into heaven and is seated at the right hand of the Father.

FROM THE NICENE CREED,
THE BOOK OF COMMON PRAYER

17

The Emperor's Vision

Having canceled the written code, with its regulations, that was against
us and that stood opposed to us; he took it away, nailing it to the cross.
And having disarmed the powers and authorities, he made a public spectacle
of them, triumphing over them by the cross. —COLOSSIANS 2:14-15

The *Chi-Rho* Cross

As he aged, Constantine the Great, like anyone else, probably wanted to make sense of his life and accomplishments. To ensure a place in history, the fourth-century emperor enlisted the historian Eusebius as his confessor and scribe. Among the stories, Constantine recounted his victory over Maxentius at the Milvian Bridge, a pivotal juncture in Christian and world history.

As Constantine prepared to battle Maxentius for control of the Roman Empire, a vision startled him. According to Eusebius, "[Constantine] said that about noon, when the day was already beginning to decline, he saw with his own eyes the trophy of a cross of light in the heavens, above the sun, and bearing the inscription, CONQUER BY

THIS. At this sight he himself was struck with amazement, and his whole army also, which followed him on this expedition, and witnessed the miracle."

After the apparition, Constant doubted its validity. So that night, "God appeared to him with the same sign which he had seen in the heavens, and commanded him to make a likeness of that sign . . . and to use it as a safeguard in all engagements with is enemies." The sign was the *Chi-Rho* monogram, also known as a Christogram, superimposing the first two letters of Christ's name in Greek.

The next morning Constantine called in his metalworkers and goldsmiths. He "sat in the mist of them" and described the sign. Then they began working.

The Standard of the Cross

Eusebius recorded how Constantine's "workers in gold and precious stones" made a standard with the *Chi-Rho* symbol, later called the "Labarum." His description details the banner's beauty and precision, along with a royal regard for this sign of the cross:

A long spear, overlaid with gold, formed the figure of the cross by means of a transverse bar laid over it. On the top of the whole was fixed a wreath of gold and precious stones; and within this, the Saviour's name, two letters indicating the name of Christ by means of its initial characters, the letter P being intersected by X in the centre: and these letters the emperor was in the habit of wearing on his helmet at a later period.

From the cross-bar of the spear was suspended a cloth, a royal piece, covered with a profuse embroidery of most brilliant precious stones; and which, being also richly interlaced with gold, presented an indescribable degree of beauty to the beholder. The banner was square in form, and the upright staff, whose lower section was of great length, bore a portrait of the pious emperor and his children on its upper part, beneath the trophy of the cross, and immediately above the embroidered banner.

The emperor constantly made use of this sign of salvation as a safeguard against every adverse and hostile power, and commanded that others similar to it should be carried at the head of all armies.

Constantine carried the banner into battle and won. Eusebius compared the victory to Moses and the Israelites safely crossing the Red Sea while the pharaoh's army faltered and drowned. Constantine rescued Christians from persecution by declaring their religion legal, and changed the spiritual trajectory of the vast Roman world. Among his many accomplishments, he protected and supported the church, especially by instigating an ambitious church-building program, and called together the Council of Nicea that solidified the faith's fundamental beliefs. He opened the door for Emperor Theodosius to declare Christianity the state religion in the fifth century. When Constantine moved his capital to Constantinople, the Byzantines considered him the founder of Eastern Christianity. Throughout the empire, the *Chi-Rho* served as his imperial sign of the cross.

The Sincerity of Conversion

Historians debate whether Constantine sincerely converted to Christianity or just used the religion to build his ego and influence. He still paid homage to the pagan sun god during his reign, dealt ruthlessly with enemies and waited until his deathbed to be baptized. Some think the emperor gradually became a Christian over the years. Despite the debate about his personal beliefs, Christianity and signs of the cross endured because of his powerful and aggressive influence.

The *Chi-Rho* sign also thrived, taking on visual variations as it passed through the hands of artisans in successive eras and locations. Eventually Constantine's sign of the cross commonly appeared with the Greek letters *alpha* and *omega*. Or less frequently, the *ichthus*, the Christian sign of the fish. At times the vertical bar has transformed into a staff, an anchor, a nail, a letter and other meaningful symbols. The entire monogram has been wreathed, framed, encircled and sur-rounded with vines. Overall, professional artists and laypeople have drawn, carved, painted, fused, engraved, doodled and scratched the *Chi-Rho* as an expression of faith, permeating every form of Christian art. The emperor's vision, the sign in the sky, is as recognizable today as seventeen centuries ago.

One look at a cross altered the world. Encountering the cross can still change hearts today.

18

Searching for the Real Thing

May I never boast except in the cross of our
Lord Jesus Christ, through which the world has been
crucified to me, and I to the world. —GALATIANS 6:14

Crucifixion Nails

IN THE FOURTH CENTURY, Empress Helena was a woman on a mission. When her son, Emperor Constantine, ordered the excavation of the Holy Sepulcher site, she traveled to Jerusalem. Constantine wanted to destroy the pagan Temple of Venus built over Christ's tomb and replace it with a church. But before the construction began, Helena directed the workers to dig deep and uncover any remains in this hallowed place. According to Christian tradition, they found a sepulcher, three crosses, nails and the titulus from Jesus' crucifixion. Helena rejoiced and instigated a consecration ceremony for the True Cross. Later Ambrose, bishop of Milan in the fourth century, preached that when Helena discovered the cross "she worshiped not the wood but the King, him who hung on the wood. She burned with an earnest desire of touching the guarantee of immortality."

Afterward, the empress donated a section of the cross and Christ's titilus to Jerusalem, and church leaders encased them for safekeeping. Helena returned to Constantinople with the cross remains and the nails. Constantine privately enclosed a piece of the cross in the monumental statue of himself in the Forum at Constantinople. Craftsmen incorporated the nails into Constantine's helmet and his horse's bridle, and some church fathers considered the bridle's ornamentation a fulfillment of Zechariah's prophecy: "In that day that which is upon the bridle of the horse shall be holy to the Lord" (Zech 14:20 Douay-Rheims Bible).

Interest in the True Cross

Over several centuries, the spreading story of Helena's quest turned legendary and fueled an extreme preoccupation with the True Cross. Christians from everywhere wanted to see, touch or obtain at least a sliver of this wood. Toward the end of the fourth century, bishop Cyril of Jerusalem described an incident that typified this interest. In Jerusalem on Good Friday, Christians gathered in the Chapel of the Cross, built near the Calvary site, to honor Christ's cross. After the bishop stretched his hand over the cross fragment, believers filed past it, with deacons maintaining the ceremony's orderliness. However, leaders banned worshipers from touching the wood with their hands. At one point, though, an enterprising man outwitted the system and bit off a piece of the sacred wood. Sources are unclear about what happened to this man and his bite-sized souvenir.

Because of their prestige and popularity, slivers of the True Cross dispersed throughout Christendom. In a letter to Constantine's son and successor, Cyril of Jerusalem wrote: "He [Jesus] was truly crucified for our sins. For if you would deny it, the place refutes you visibly, this blessed Golgotha, in which we are now assembled for the sake of him who was here crucified; *and the whole world has since been filled with pieces of the wood of the Cross*" (italics added). Usually cathedrals, high church officials, royalty or the wealthy owned these bits of wood.

Through the centuries Christians hid, displayed, stole, lost, wore and gave away these wood particles.

As early as the fourth century John Chrysostom noted that Christians reverently wore True Cross fragments "upon their persons." In the fifth century, as a conciliatory gesture Juvenal, the Patriarch of Jerusalem, sent a fragment of the "precious wood" to Pope Leo I in Rome. When Radegunda, Queen of the Franks, accepted a piece of the cross from Emperor Justin II in the sixth century, she celebrated with a feast and renamed the Poitiers monastery "Holy Cross." In the ninth century Emperor Charlemagne wore a cross sliver as a talisman, encased in a pendant attached to a chain around his neck. Belief in the True Cross flourished into the Middle Ages, supported by popes, kings and patriarchs. In turn, cathedrals and parishes honored the cross with annual festivals.

Reforming Christian Beliefs

By the Reformation, claims about the True Cross and its authenticity grew enormously out of proportion. It seemed like anyone and everyone could own a sliver and claim that it held miraculous powers. A sincere desire to find Christ's cross had ballooned into a questionable industry.

In the sixteenth century the reformer John Calvin criticized the cross obsession in his popular pamphlet, "Against the Worship of Relics." Calvin refuted the claims of so many pieces of Christ's cross in the world. He complained, "Fragments of the cross found by St. Helena are scattered over many churches in Italy, France, Spain, etc., and would form a good shipload, which it would take three hundred men to carry instead of one. . . . Some affirm that their fragments were carried by angels, others that they dropped down from heaven. Those of Poitiers say that their piece was stolen by a maid-servant of Helena and carried off to France." Calvin considered these claims preposterous and mathematically infeasible.

He also confronted the incredulity of the number of Holy Nails. Tradition accepted that Helena found three nails, but Calvin exposed "a greater controversy as to the three nails of the cross: one of them was fixed in the crown of Constantine, the other two were fitted to his horse's bridle, according to Theodoret, or one was kept by Helena herself, according to Ambrose. But now there are two nails at Rome, one at Siena, one at Milan, one at Carpentras, one at Venice, one at Cologne, one at Treves, two at Paris, one at Bourges, etc. All the claims are equally good, for the nails are all spurious."

Calvin exaggerated about the shipload of wood, but his point stuck. Belief in the True Cross staggered and cracked under the weight of the reformers' attacks, and Protestants expressed their disbelief. For them, Helena's story turned to ashes, although belief in the True Cross lingers today.

Looking for the Authentic

I'd never heard about Helena and the True Cross until at mid-life I studied medieval art history. Because religious and royal leaders commissioned reliquaries to display at least alleged pieces of this cross, books about early Christian, Byzantine and medieval art tell the story or at least refer to it. Now as an art-history teacher, I present this anecdote to students in the context of the astonishing works of art it generated for many centuries.

On a personal level, I think searching for the True Cross illustrates our desire for the authentic. If we can touch or see something called "the real thing," this bolsters our faith. But even with sacred artifacts, locations and memorials, we can't always pinpoint the precise details or truth about everything declared Christian. Certain extrabiblical stories and artifacts are real; others are legendary and counterfeit. Sometimes it's hard to tell the difference.

Ultimately and most importantly, we live by Scripture's teachings. The New Testament says, "faith is being sure of what we hope for and certain of what we do not see. This is what the ancients were commended for" (Heb 11:1-2). As we pursue God, we live by faith, relying on the unseen. Although artifacts are interesting, they can't be our assurance. Only the Lord himself can guarantee his eternal promises.

Ultimately, I think Christ cares more about our personal authenticity than anything else. Cyprian, the third-century bishop of Carthage, told persecuted Christians, "It is written that the just live by faith. If you are just and live by faith—if you truly believe in Christ—why do you not embrace the assurance that you are called to Christ? Why do you not rejoice that you are freed from the devil?" When we focus on answering these questions, artifacts can take their appropriate place.

19

A Cross in the Desert

Jesus, full of the Holy Spirit, returned from the Jordan
and was led by the Spirit in the desert. —LUKE 4:1

**A Dome Cross at Saint
Catherine's Monastery**

A HOWLING WIND SWEEPS through the gorge, testing the will of earnest pilgrims traveling to this desolate and splendid site. Approaching the desert monastery, its impenetrable stone walls seem determined to ward off even the friendliest intruders. Only the crosses atop buildings within the fortress, peeking above the massive ramparts, urge visitors forward with a faint welcome.

Even so, pressing through the harsh isolation rewards dusty travelers beyond their weary-though-earnest expectations. The arid, rocky landscape yields to Egypt's magnificent Mount Sinai, recalling the reluctant deliverer Moses, a burning bush and stone tablets that commanded his nation's obedience. Once inside the protective walls, ancient treasures within Saint Catherine's Monastery silently witness a sacred past.

At one point a rope and a lift provided the only entrance into the monastery, protecting monks from invading Bedouins. Now an electronic whine pierces the wasteland as tourists navigate a metal detector to investigate Eastern Christianity. Saint

Saint Catherine's Monastery. Mount Sinai. Sixth century.

Catherine's celebrates fifteen hundred years as an inhabited monastery, settled in the Sinai desert, and countless visitors who've passed through its doors. Several years ago, with the help of an urban museum and modern technology, the monastery observed this anniversary by reopening its renovated Treasury, full of sacred artifacts. But the assistance of modernity hasn't changed the monastery's asceticism, with its age-old rituals of work and worship. Visitors slow down, adjust, to the quiet rhythms of monastic life.

Iconic Crosses in the Desert

Funded by Emperor Justinian in the sixth century, Saint Catherine's houses thousands of ancient Christian relics, including crosses, caskets, paintings, tapestries, reliquaries, liturgical vessels, clerical vestments and illuminated manuscripts. However, the more than two thousand icons constitute the most renowned collection in the monastery and perhaps the world. Two famous sixth- to seventh-century icons painted on wood and frequently reprinted in art books and textbooks, urge visitors to pause and contemplate the centrality of Christ and the consequences of his cross.

A well-preserved icon known as the Sinai Christ depicts an almost life-sized, bearded Christ steadily gazing at the viewer. In his left hand, he holds a Gospel book with a jeweled cross on its ornamented cover. His right hand, with the two lower fingers touching the thumb, has been interpreted as the gesture of an orator, a motion of blessing or the sign of the cross. Tradition claims that this image of the Christ Pantokrator—the "All Powerful" or "Ruler of All"—authentically represents the Savior's appearance. This is the Christ who triumphed over death and now reigns with power and authority.

Another icon, the Sinai Saint Peter, feels more sobering. Peter's slightly drooping eyes avert the viewer, communicating an unspoken sadness. His right hand holds silver keys to the kingdom of heaven, while the apostle's left hand and shoulder support a cross-staff, representing his Christ-appointed leadership on earth. Three small medallions above his head encircle Christ, his mother Mary and probably John the evangelist. In a sacred twist of irony, damages to the icon, acquired through the years, contribute to the solemnity of Peter's aged and weathered features. Lingering with the apostle, visitors reckon with the cost of his commitment to Christ and the church. Symbolically, shouldering the cross sacrificed Peter's life.

From the crosses carved on the south wall facing Moses' mountain to the many small and unexpected spaces displaying them, Saint Catherine's invites visitors and residents to consider the monastery's original purpose. It sheltered monastics who wanted to follow the way of Christ and his cross. Saint Isaac, a seventh-century Syrian monastic, explained, "The knowledge of the Cross is concealed in the sufferings of the Cross." With similar intent, the world's oldest working monastery and smallest diocese still assists those called to the desert's solitude and afflictions.

The Call of the Desert

Like Jesus who roamed alone for forty days, the desert's severity wooed early Christians who wanted to separate from the crowd, control their passions and perpetually seek God. Even before the third-century Saint Anthony, considered the father of Christian monasticism, the wadi and rocks hosted hermits and their peculiar devotion to Christ. Gradually, caves with lone occupants conceded to monastic communities that fed, sheltered and promoted the pursuit of holiness.

Yet even in community, desert monasticism swallowed up a life, balancing sheer survival with a demanding spirituality. A nineteenth-century monastic, St. Theophan the Recluse, explained, "Monasticism itself is a perpetual labor of conquering passions and uprooting them in order that, being in a pure and immaculate state, one may preserve oneself before the face of God." This was—and still is—the monastic way of following Christ's cross into the desert.

Most of us, though, live in contrast to the desert monk. Even if handed the opportunity, many of us would decline the hypnotic, heat-worn days of such strenuous solitude. Or at least I would. Then again, I periodically journey into my own personal wastelands, fraught with emotional and spiritual desolation. As I've grown older I've learned that solitude can be exactly what I need: a time of limited isolation to mentally take shelter from the whipping wind, quiet the howling in my head and hope for the sandstorm to settle. Even if it's just for an hour by myself or only a space inside my soul. Metaphorically, I stake a cross in the desert and wait for Christ to appear.

Personal deserts require the "perpetual labor" of waiting for the Lord. Scripture encourages us with the psalmist's guidance: "Wait on the LORD: be of good courage, and he shall strengthen thine heart: wait, I say, on the LORD" (Ps 27:14 KJV). And so, with inner solitude, we wait for the sign of his cross.

20

The Missionary Cross

And the gospel must first be preached to all nations. —MARK 13:10

The Cross of Muiredach

A<small>CCORDING TO</small> I<small>RISH LEGEND</small>, the sixth-century monk Columba admired and apparently needed the *Cathach,* a psalter from the late sixth or seventh century, for his mission work and personal piety. (Or maybe he simply coveted the ornate book? In an era of illiteracy, owning an illuminated manuscript signified prestige.) Whatever the motivation, Columba copied the psalter without permission from the monastic leader Finnian, the manuscript's owner. This devalued the book artistically and financially, so Finnian appealed to High King Dermott who declared, "to every cow its calf; to every book its copy" and ordered Columba to relinquish the copy.

With a large dose of hubris Columba refused and Dermott declared war. Although Columba's family won by tromping Dermott's forces at the Battle of Cooldrevny, the strong-willed monk damaged his soul. Marauding over a psalm book wasn't behavior fit for a priest who reportedly introduced Christ's cross to the Celts and founded several monasteries. Columba's spiritual mentor, Molaisi of Devenish, banished him to Iona. As penance, Molaisi instructed Columba to convert as many people to Christ as those who'd died in the battle over a psalm book. Consequently, in his early forties Columba took twelve monks with him and founded another monastery in the land of the Picts, whom the Romans called "the painted ones."

Reading the account of Columba's life, crossing the waters to Iona affected more than a change of location. After this journey, stories about Columba emphasized his holiness and powerful ministry characterized by miracles. According to Abbott Adamnan's *Life of Columba,* Columba traveled to the mainland and scared off the Loch Ness Monster by making the sign of the cross. This courageous act impressed the Picts and they converted to Christianity.

Written in the seventh century from oral histories, the biography also described how Columba relied on the cross for other miracles, such as chasing off a demon, transforming people, blessing objects, empowering a boat's sails and blasting open bolted doors. Although stories about Columba turned mythic, crosses throughout the British Isles witness to his spiritual zeal. After Columba's death, Christians referred to the Celtic cross as Columba's cross or the Ionic cross, named after his monastery.

The Celtic cross also recalls Patrick of Armagh, the earlier, fifth-century missionary to Ireland. Folklore abounds about this revered missionary, although scant historical literature exists to confirm his true biography. However, it's believable that Patrick relied on Christ's cross in his missionary endeavors. This excerpt from "The Lorica," Saint Patrick's prayer for protection, reveals his belief in the crucifixion's power as he evangelized a pagan, superstitious culture.

I bind to myself today
The virtue of the Incarnation of Christ with His Baptism,

The virtue of His crucifixion with His burial,
The virtue of His Resurrection with His Ascension,
The virtue of His coming on the Judgement Day.

Wheels of Stone and Glory

In the tradition of Columba and Patrick, stone carvers erected Celtic crosses in northern England, Ireland and Scotland from the eighth through tenth centuries. These crosses comprised the largest group of freestanding sculpture between the Roman Empire and the Renaissance's Italian city-states. Celtic crosses marked gravesites, monasteries, outdoor Mass sites and important crossroads. They also commemorated events, saints or other individuals. Some served devotional or penitential purposes for the pious and the repentant.

Ireland added the distinctive "wheels of glory" that identify Celtic crosses. On these crosses, a wheel connected the four arms, creating a stylized version of their Latin counterpart. Several theories suggest the origin of these wheels: a pagan reference to the sun, a Christian processional cross or the wreathed cross of late antiquity. In addition to the wheels, sculptors also carved Celtic crosses with Christian images, narratives, symbols and inscriptions on the front, back and sides. Sometimes they also incorporated pagan and cultural images, or abstractions, depending on whether a group was fully or partially evangelized.

Ireland boasts the biggest number of wheel crosses, and many can be observed up close and touched. Generally, art observers consider the early tenth-century Cross of Muiredach at Monasterboice, Louth County, in Ireland one of the finest examples of the Celtic cross and incomparable in Europe. Carved in sandstone and eighteen feet tall, its figures can still be identified, despite centuries of harsh weather. The central carvings stand out as highlights, positioned simultaneously in the middle of the wheels of glory and the cross section of the two beams. The relief sculpture on the east face depicts lance holders, sponge bearers and angels surrounding Christ on his cross. The west face illustrates the Last Judgement, with Christ separating the "saved" from the "lost" and pronouncing their eternal destiny, a popular image during the Middle Ages. Stone carvers decorated the rest of the cross with scenes from Scripture and the lives of saints.

Other excellent Celtic examples are the South Cross of Ahenny in Tipperary County and the high crosses at Moone County, Kildare. These sturdy crosses, and many others, prevail as memorials to missionary quests in Ireland.

The Evangelistic Cross

At the end of the seventh century, Pope Gregory I sent the monk Augustine to Kent to convert the Anglo-Saxon ruler King Æthelbert. The historian Bede recorded that the king arranged to meet Augustine outdoors in case he possessed magical powers. With a similar precaution, the missionaries arrived "bearing a silver cross for their banner, and the image of our Lord and Saviour painted on a panel. They chanted litanies and uttered prayers to the Lord for their own eternal salvation and the salvation of those for whom and to whom they had come."

Hopefully, Augustine carried the cross not just for papal authority and God's protection, but also to herald his salvation message. Earlier Augustine had delivered a promise to Æthelbert through interpreters, stating he had "come from Rome bearing the best of news, namely the sure and certain promise of eternal joys in heaven and an endless Kingdom with the living and true God."

Like the enduring stone crosses, missionary history testifies to both the marvelous and misguided missions to evangelize the world. Along with Columba, as we carry the gospel to hearts and heartlands, "[H]ere is a trustworthy saying that deserves full acceptance: Christ Jesus came into the world to save sinners—of whom I am the worst" (1 Tim 1:15). Always and always, true conversion bows to the Christ of the Cross.

21

Becoming More Christian

*Do not conform any longer to the pattern of this world, but be
transformed by the renewing of your mind.* —ROMANS 12:2

The Cross Slab at Aberlemno

THE ANGLO-SAXONS OF GREAT BRITAIN enjoyed a good riddle.
When they converted to Christianity, this mind-bender form of pagan
entertainment accompanied them. A book of poetry from the tenth
century, the *Book of Exeter*, intrigued readers with the following description, known as Riddle 30. A twentieth century translator suggested this Christian interpretation.

> I am agile of body, I sport with the breeze; [tree]
> I am clothed with beauty, a comrade of the storm; [tree]
> I am bound on a journey, consumed by fire; [ship, tree]
> A burning grove, a burning gleed. [tree, log]
> Full often comrades pass me from hand to hand, [harp]
> Where stately men and women kiss me. [cup?]
> When I rise up, before me bow

The proud with reverence. Then it is my part
To increase for many the growth of happiness.
The answer: The cross.

When migratory tribes infiltrated their conquered territories, they influenced not just the customs and language, but also the arts. Often referred to as "barbarians," these tribes had developed an intricate visual art style, rich in stone, precious jewels and metalwork. As the many tribes converted to Christianity, their artistry infiltrated sculpture, jewelry, illuminated manuscripts and other creative expressions of their new faith. However, the artistic and lifestyle conversion wasn't clear-cut. For many years pagan and Christian symbols melded together as converts adjusted to altered beliefs and behaviors. This fusion of style, content and symbolism integrated into a unique expression of life and faith.

Pagan and Christian Combinations

When Scotland's forbearers, the Picts, began making crosses, they carved on boulders and stone slabs left in their natural state, mastering a fascinating form of outdoor sculpture. An eighth-century slab in Aberlemno, Scotland, exemplifies this type of carving and a dynamic syncretism of pagan and Christian symbols. The circles, spirals, interlaced lines and curvilinear beasts of migratory art embellish a Christian cross on the slab's front. The back of the slab memorializes a hunt scene and unidentified Pictish symbols.

In another curious mixture, the Papil Stone from the seventh or eighth century, housed at the National Museum of Scotland, divides into three registers or horizontal bands. The top register highlights a compass-drawn cross flanked by hooded figures carrying crosiers. The middle register frames a lion, the symbol of Mark the evangelist, with a distinctive Pictish emphasis on spiral joints and a curling tongue and tail. In the bottom register, two bird-headed men holding axes peck at or hold a small, round object. In the pagan tradition, is the round object the head of a conquered enemy? Or in the Christian tradition, is it the Eucharist Host? It's been interpreted both ways.

Scholars haven't fully unraveled the meaning of Pict images. Yet even without a complete interpretation, these cross carvings represent a Christianity that incorporated ancient beliefs, indicating a partially evangelized culture still clinging to its pagan roots. Over hundreds of years, this eclectic pattern repeated itself in the cultures that converted to Christianity. It took time for minds, hearts, customs, lifestyles and artwork to "become more Christian."

The Marauding Vikings

In the tradition of the Vikings, at the end of the tenth century the Danish King Harald Bluetooth commissioned a picture stone, a boulder with figural carvings, for his family's burial grounds near Jelling, Denmark. The stone still stands today. Its inscription reads: "King Harald had this memorial made for Gorm his father and Thyra his mother; that Harald who won for himself all Denmark and Norway and made the Danes Christians." On the front of the eight-foot stone, a sculptor carved a Byzantine-garbed Christ with his arms outstretched. But instead of hanging from a beam, interlacing ribbons wrap around the Savior's arms. A great beast prowls another side of the stone, fighting a snake and sprouting foliage from his tail and other body parts. He symbolizes the Lion of Judah.

Around this time in the British Isles and Scandinavia, secular carvers wrapped ribbon interlacing and simple foliage around recognizable animals, instead of creating the grotesque beasts of earlier Viking ships. The Jelling stone marked a transition from paganism to Christianity. A few yards away, a shorter stone honors Queen Thyra, erected by King Gorm, the last pagan king of Denmark. Pagan and Christian stand together.

During the ninth century, pagan Vikings had raided churches for their liturgical treasures and either slaughtered Christians or captured them. These raids prompted a prayer for protection in the *Antiphonary of Charles the Bald*. The prayer implored, "Pity [us] the highest favor by preserving and guarding our bodies, free us from the savage Norman tribe who devastates our realms. The aged and young would have their throats slit, and maidens and lads too, and the multitudes also. Repel the evil from us, we altogether implore [thee]." By the tenth century, Vikings abandoned the pagan ritual of burying grave goods with their dead—an archaeological sign that Christianity had taken root. Viking coins bore signs of the cross. The captive had converted their captors.

Slow but Sure Transitions

Over time, migratory tribes transformed into medieval Christian cultures. Yet if we'd judged by their initial transition to Christianity, we'd consider the conversions a failure or at least questionable. Mixing beliefs and symbology doesn't conform to our definition of true Christianity. Contemporary Western culture prefers efficient, clean transitions, with no jagged remains left behind. Even in conversions to the faith, we want an immediate renunciation of former beliefs, immersion in the Christian culture and rapid spiritual growth. But wisdom and experience teach us otherwise.

The total work of the cross requires time and patience. Although a confession of faith might be quick, with sins immediately forgiven, genuine sanctification lasts a lifetime. Ancient cultures suggest that slow change can foster lasting transformation. We can draw from this principle if we guide the spiritual transformation of others. We can bestow this patience on ourselves.

PART FIVE

Daily Signs of Salvation

The Cross in Ancient Everyday Life

[In early Christianity], crosses decorated many daily objects: They were carved or painted on the facades of private and public buildings, erected in fields and on roadsides, and stamped on eating utensils. This sign was especially common on oil lamps, perhaps as a symbolic means of banishing the darkness. . . . In addition, it served as an official mark of reliability and honesty, appearing on weights and, of course, on most Byzantine Imperial coins. The cross was believed to be an effective form of defense against Satan and the forces of evil and was therefore made into jewelry, which was worn by the living as amulets.

THE CRADLE OF CHRISTIANITY EXHIBIT
THE ISRAEL MUSEUM, JERUSALEM

22

A Cross for the Darkness

You, O LORD, keep my lamp burning; my God turns my darkness into light. —PSALM 18:28

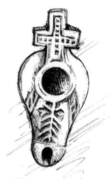

Oil Lamp with Cross

Several years ago I visited a one-room biblical archaeology museum attached to a small Christian university. The docent fascinated our group with ancient artifacts, handing them out so we could touch Scripture's history. I remember examining a clay pot and holding facsimiles of iron nails used for a Roman crucifixion. The spike-sized nails evoked murmurs as they passed from one person to another, but the object that stirred me most slipped into my hands quietly. *It's so small,* I thought. The archaic oil lamp, in remarkably good condition, fit in the palm of my hand.

While reading biblical metaphors about oil lamps, or looking at them in museum catalogs, I'd imagined vessels much larger than this. How did a traveler find his way in the darkness with such a tiny, fluttering flame? How did a mother sweep a floor, straighten the house or snuggle her children into bed? My American expectations loomed large for light sources after sundown: floodlights, searchlights, spotlights, streetlights, ceiling lights with whirling fans. Obviously, these people knew something more than I did—something wise and almost mysterious—about navigating the night.

Later I thought about Old and New Testament references to lamplight. The Israelite psalmist wrote, "Your word is a lamp to my feet / and a light for my path" (Ps 119:105). An ancient proverb claimed, "The light of the righteous shines brightly, but the lamp of the wicked is snuffed out" (Prov 13:9). While telling the parable about a woman who lost a coin, Jesus asked, "Does she not light a lamp, sweep the house and search carefully until she finds it?" (Lk 15:8). Most likely, early Christians understood lamp metaphors in practical ways unfamiliar to me. Every day in shadowy rooms, every evening when the sun descended, they lit oil lamps to illumine shades of darkness.

Carving Out Religious Beliefs

For thousands of years before Christ, oil lamps served as light sources for civilizations. However, pottery lamps didn't flourish until about the eighth or seventh century BC. These simple, wheel-thrown vessels looked like saucers with turned-up edges, with wicks immersed in olive or vegetable oil and draped over the edges. Later the Greeks innovated by enclosing their lamps and adding spouts, handles and glazes. During the Hellenistic Age and the early centuries of Christianity, lamps created from moulds of clay, stone or plaster dispersed as much as those shaped on pottery wheels. Aside from increasing production, moulds allowed elaborate designs and three-dimensional figures to appear on lamps created for religious ceremonies or wealthy patrons. At the same time, factories mass produced undecorated lamps, either for humble homes or Jews whose religious tradition prohibited graven images. Pottery makers stamped the bottom of these popular *firmalampen* with the factory owner's name. Archaeologists today still unearth these stamped lamps throughout the former Roman Empire while digging up settlements and burial sites.

The Herodian lamp —named after the reign of Herod the Great—populated Palestine's hill country and cities from about 50 BC to AD 70. It's possible this lamp evolved in Jerusalem or a nearby location. To

Early Christian oil lamps. The Israel Museum, Jerusalem. Fifth through seventh centuries.

create the Herodian lamp, potters shaped a circular, wheel-made body with a wide spout applied by hand. A hole in the middle of the base accommodated filling the lamp with oil, and the spout's opening held the wick and its flame. Jesus probably envisioned this lamp when he told the parable about ten maidens waiting for the bridegroom (Mt 25:1-13), or explained to his listeners, "You are the light of the world. A city on a hill cannot be hidden. Neither do people light a lamp and put it under a bowl. Instead they put it on its stand, and it gives light to everyone in the house" (Mt 5:14-15). Because of their familiarity, oil lamps served as effective spiritual metaphors.

Almost two millennia later, oil lamps help archaeologists pinpoint ancient Christian activity. In late antiquity, oils lamps often expressed religious beliefs with symbols or inscriptions. Pottery workshops in Cyprus, Greece, Egypt, North Africa and Syria-Palestine manufactured lamps portraying pagan gods, Jewish menorahs and Christian crosses. When archaeologists recover lamps with crosses, they tentatively assume a Christian community resided nearby. For example, researchers discovered lamps with crosses in an ancient funerary complex at Tel el-Fûl, north of Jerusalem. The crosses indicated that Christians settled in that area sixteen hundred years ago.

Lamps with crosses flooded the Roman Empire in the fourth and fifth centuries, after Christianity became the religion of emperors. Constantine's monogram of the cross, the Christogram, was a favorite symbol, either stamped on a lamp's body or extended as the handle. Art historians theorize that these crosses symbolized the banishment of spiritual darkness.

It's an apt interpretation. As early Christians held out their lamps and stepped carefully into the darkness, they could see crosses guiding them. Literally, the sign of the cross was a light for their paths. But even more, Christ's cross shed light on their world's spiritually dark places.

Shining into a Dark World

"The mystery of the cross shines bright," wrote the bishop of Poitiers in the sixth century. Listening to the newscasts, we might wonder about the veracity of that long-ago claim. The world seems full of so much darkness. But in our frustration, we can recall early Christians carrying their oil lamps, following the flickering cross-flames before them, casting light on their paths with each footfall. Perhaps they modeled how we can shed light into our world: not with bonfire ideas that blast into the darkness and eventually fade into cinders, but by faithfully inching along in the world's darkness, extending the light of the cross to fulfill Isaiah's prophecy: "The people living in darkness / have seen a great light; / on those living in the land of the shadow of death / a light has dawned" (Mt 4:16). They would see the light of the cross.

Recently I purchased an inexpensive replica of an ancient oil lamp from a workshop in Crete. The lamp sits on my desk and its imprinted cross points at me while I work. It reminds me of the lamplight promises of Scripture. When I need to believe the cross can shine light into any darkness, I can light a lamp.

23

Hoping for the Cross

*Faith is being sure of what we hope for and
certain of what we do not see.* —HEBREWS 11:1

The Rotas-Sator Square

WHEN MOUNT VESUVIUS EXPLODED in AD 79, the scorching lava
buried Pompeii and its residents who didn't escape. This is a docu-
mented fact, taught to students as early as grade school. Yet many of
us overlook that Vesuvius also destroyed Herculaneum, a nearby
town. For several decades archaeologists have dug into the accumu-
lated earth of both settlements, excavating well-preserved people,
places and things from the ashes. Over time, one culture's tragedy
hardened into another civilization's treasure.

Pompeii and Herculaneum teach us about first-century Roman life.
But sometimes these revelations also dash our hopes. For example, a
second-floor apartment in Herculaneum housed a rectangular wall
covered with white plaster. Upon discovery, it looked as though an
ancient Roman engraved a Latin cross in the plaster. Researchers in-

terpreted a nearby chest as an altar, and decided the room was a Christian place of worship. This discovery reportedly proved that Christians lived in Herculaneum. However, further exploration suggested that wooden brackets for a wall cabinet or shelf, with a supporting upright piece, left the imprint. Excavators, perhaps eager to make a new discovery, had hoped for a cross.

Not far away in Pompeii, archaeologists found a square-shaped acrostic inscription in two homes. The letters arranged as follows in Latin:

R O T A S
O P E R A
T E N E T
A R E P O
S A T O R

Over the years scholars have ventured various interpretations of the square, emphasizing a reference to the "sower" and his "plough." From an early time, Christians referred to Christ as the Sower so it seemed plausible that the Rotas-Sator Square disguised a Christian message. With closer inspection, some scholars deciphered that the word square's letters rearranged into two crosses, both composed of the opening words of the Lord's Prayer (*Pater Noster* or "Our Father"). They thought the remaining letters, two sets of *A* and *O,* stood for Christ who is the *Alpha* and *Omega,* the beginning and the end.

However, after more investigation, scholars disagreed whether the Christian arrangement was intended or coincidental. Equally compelling arguments pointed to the acrostic's Jewish and Mithraic origins. (Some first-century Romans worshiped the Persian bull-slaying god, Mithras.) But if someone embedded the cross within this ancient word square, he emphasized the deep-seated desire for symbolism in early Christianity. The house's occupants would have considered this acrostic a blessing on their family. If the cross was coincidental, the discovery highlighted modernity's desire to validate ancient Christianity. It

would have been spiritually and intellectually invigorating to confirm the presence of Christians in Pompeii.

Along with these controversial cross discoveries, scholars have offered alternate explanations for other "evidence" of Christianity in Herculaneum and Pompeii, creating academic disputes. Some believe Christians inhabited these locations; others do not. This uncertainty extends into other revelations from early Christianity. Sometimes experts can precisely identify the meaning and authenticity of symbols, objects or artwork. Other times, they can only speculate.

Recognizing What's Not There

Excavating ancient Christian symbols and artifacts causes a stir. Archaeologists, art historians and other scholars delight in an unexpected "find." Even small shards from an archaeological dig can fill blank spaces in the puzzle called ancient cultures, corroborating or disproving what researchers suspect. Unearthing authentic, early symbols of Christianity especially encourages the worldwide community of believers, affirming our faith. But when we delve into these ancient mysteries, hard facts and educated guesses can also challenge our preconceived notions. Some initial assumptions about early Christianity don't prove true. As much as we want to see a cross, it's simply not there.

I'm not a researcher, but I think backtracking and recognizing what doesn't exist could be an archaeologist's lesson in humility. But it's also the avenue for starting over, looking for what's true. Inspired explorers redirect their efforts, trying again and again, still hoping to find what they desire.

These researchers also offer a spiritual metaphor to us. We'd like to observe the cross in our daily lives, pointing to its loving and sacrificial influence. But sometimes it's just not visible. We want to be servant leaders. We crave safety and kindness in family life. We hope to ignore the pushiness of addictions. We intend to greet needy people with patience and compassion. We try not to criticize and judge. But somehow our behaviors don't reflect Christ's cross. Managing our everyday lives, we recognize its regrettable absence.

Thankfully, admitting the truth can redirect the heart and stir up a fresh search. Jesus emphasized that when we search, we will find. We can welcome the life-changing cross we hoped for.

24

Fear No Evil

*Since the children have flesh and blood, he too shared in their
humanity so that by his death he might destroy him who holds the
power of death—that is, the devil—and free those who all their lives
were held in slavery by their fear of death.* —HEBREWS 2:14-15

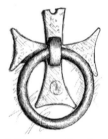

A Cross Door Knocker

A STONE SLAB DECORATED WITH A CROSS and unearthed in Nizzana,
Israel, proclaims, "Christ wins, Christ reigns. Stephen of Patricius
made [this] in the month of Loos, in the tenth year of the indiction.
May the envious burst!"

Carved in the sixth century, the slab immortalizes the early Christian belief in the cross's spiritual victory. Many early Christians believed
that when Christ died, he broke the power of Satan and his minions, and
the sign of their Savior's cross warded off the world's evils. As a result,
followers of Jesus displayed his cross in a variety of community settings.
They painted crosses on building facades, erected them in fields and
built them along roadsides. They believed a doorknocker in the form of
a cross, on a public or private building, protected the people within.

The cross's protective power also extended to individuals. Christians took seriously Christ's power over sin and death, and they extended that belief to their everyday lives. They also remembered the psalmist's claim, "I will fear no evil, for you are with me" (Ps 23:4). As a result, these believers wore cross pendants and amulets not only for adornment, but to protect them from evil.

An amulet is "an object that by its nearness to a person who possesses it keeps evil away or brings good luck." Amulets originally thrived in Hellenistic-Roman religions as a means of magic. They were made from animal or vegetable matter, written on papyrus or carved on stone or metal. Frequently, amulets bore the inscription, "Protect from every evil," although some carried specific or mysterious requests. Romans hoped amulets would deflect curses, spells and other harms against them. Many Christians adopted amulets to display the cross, expressing their faith in its protective influence.

Averting the Evil Eye

In the fourth century the presbyter Basil of Caesarea wrote his homily *On Envy* probably as a response to problems within his parish. Basil addressed a close-knit community with plenty of opportunity for comparison and envy. He explained, "For thus it is. The Scythian does not cast the evil eye at the Egyptian at all, but *at his own kind.* Among those he knows best, he did not envy those he did not know, *but his closest intimates,* his neighbors, and those of the same trade, those of the same age, his relatives, and brothers."

Basil's reference to "the evil eye" wasn't an angry look or just a creative phrase, as we might think of it today. For over a millennium eastern Mediterranean cultures had believed in the debilitating effects of the evil eye, a look of envy cast from one person to another. According to this belief, an envious look—whether an unintentional gaze or an intentional glare—destroyed the success or health of the envied person. If a neighbor complimented a person's appearance, family or possessions, this predicted calamity upon the person or his household. Consequently, to protect themselves, people wore amulets around their necks or hidden in clothes to ward off the evil eye.

Basil counteracted belief in the evil eye, teaching his congregation that the devil instigated envy, and this sin could be overcome by virtue. He wrote, "If you strive for the [proper] glory, and you are both eager to be above envious people, and because of this will not tolerate being second-rate (for this is an attack of envy), then, like a stream, change yourself by love of honor towards the acquisition of virtue." Later he added, "In just this way you will save yourself, and the more good you do the more you will have." Basil's advice applied to both the envious and the envied in his congregation.

We don't know if Basil's audience followed his counsel, but some early Christians wore pendant crosses or amulets decorated with crosses to avert the evil eye. They also wore or carried small mirrors, adorned with crosses, to deflect envious stares. This practice extended into Byzantium. Even though Christians embraced the cross, some still clung to a few cultural superstitions. Ancient artifacts created to stave off the evil eye illustrate the earnest syncretism of these early Christians. They mixed together old and new beliefs: pagan, Jewish and Christian.

The Common Fear Factor

Today we classify amulets and the evil eye as superstitions, misguided beliefs of Christians migrating away from paganism. Even so, we can reach back and empathize with their feelings. All cultures fear harm and loss, seeking ways to calm and resolve their anxieties, to protect themselves and others, to ward off evil when it approaches or overcomes us. In the face of fear, Scripture teaches us to trust in the Lord, not the tokens or symbols that represent him. When we display a cross, it's not the sign that saves us; it's the power of God shared by Christ who died on the cross.

I descend from a complicated line of worried women, and as a young girl I inherited the propensity to fear. My mother comforted me with scraps of paper, quoting verses like "When I am afraid, I will trust in you" (Ps 56:3) or "The LORD is with me; I will not be afraid. What can man do to me?" (Ps 118:6). Most of the things I worried about never happened, but I still carried fearfulness into adulthood, disguised as denial or "concerns." But deep down, I knew I could fear both the realistic and the ridiculous.

I talked to God when I felt afraid, but reading or "praying" the psalms especially helped. David the psalmist assured me:

> The LORD is my light and my salvation—
>   whom shall I fear?
> The LORD is the stronghold of my life—
>   of whom shall I be afraid? . . .
> For in the day of trouble
>   he will keep me safe in his dwelling;
> he will hide me in the shelter of his tabernacle
>   and set me high upon a rock. . . .
> I am still confident of this:
>   I will see the goodness of the LORD
>   in the land of the living. (Ps 27:1, 5, 13)

These days, because of my interest in Christian art and symbolism, I'm comforted by praying with a cross in my hands. For me, it represents God's sacrifice for his people, his power to rescue us and his admonition to fear not. At the same time, I understand if we gaze upon a cross symbol or hold a cross replica when we pray, it's only a symbol. It's Christ who holds the power. It's the Lord who said, "It is I; don't be afraid" (Jn 6:20).

25

The Trustworthy Standard

Here is a trustworthy saying: If we died with him,
we will also live with him; if we endure, we will
also reign with him. —2 TIMOTHY 2:11-12

A Petrie Weight
with a Wreathed Cross

D o you have grain? I'll trade it for the oil I need." The earliest
cultures practiced a barter economy, trading for goods instead of ex-
changing money. But as societies grew more complex and trade
reached across borders, cities and nations needed a standardized trade
value. Even so, groups set up their own standards of weights and measures, and confusion clogged business dealings between cities, dis-
tricts and cultures.

Eventually ancient Eastern governments introduced the balance
scale to determine weights. This scale "consisted of a beam supported
in the middle with a pan suspended by cords on each end. A known
quantity of weight would be placed in the pan on one side of the balance and the object to be weighed on the other side. By adding or re-

moving known weights until each side was equal, the weight of the object could be determined."

Made from stone or metal, craftsmen carved the weights into many shapes: cones, cubes, cylinders, domes, spheres, gods or animals such as ducks, lions or turtles. But even though artisans created pleasing forms, they seldom inscribed the weights with their value. A shopper often couldn't determine the size of a vendor's weight. As a result, many buyers carried their own weights in pouches, both to monitor unscrupulous vendors and because values varied from one location to another. Using a balance with the buyer's weights increased the likelihood of the desired amount and a fair value.

The business of weights and measures could be tricky, and the potential for scams didn't escape God's notice. When the Lord handed laws to the Israelites, he warned, "Do not have two differing weights in your bag—one heavy, one light. Do not have two differing measures in your house—one large, one small. You must have accurate and honest weights and measures, so that you may live long in the land the LORD your God is giving you. For the LORD your God detests anyone who does these things, anyone who deals dishonestly" (Deut 25:13-16). He wanted his people to be trustworthy.

Later the proverb writer echoed this instruction: "Honest scales and balances are from the LORD; all the weights in the bag are of his making. Kings detest wrongdoing, for a throne is established through righteousness" (Prov 16:11-12).

Early Christian Transactions

Carrying God's warning into early Christianity, the cross became an official symbol meant to assure quality and reputable business transactions. Bronze weights with crosses promised fairness and honesty while weighing goods for sale. Sometimes these symbols of reliability could be elaborate. For example, a circa fifth- to sixth-century bronze weight from the Beth Shean Valley, near the Sea of Galilee, depicts a cross inside a shrine. But in most cases, the design was simple. Either way, purchasers could rely on the sign of the cross. It indicated a trustworthy standard.

The balance scale and its weights enjoyed a long life, used by Early Christian, medieval, Byzantine and later cultures. In a copy of the Byzantine *Homilies of Gregory Nazianzus,* painted sometime between the eleventh and fourteenth century, a miniature painting illustrates a tax collector at work. In "The Payment of Taxes," a tax collector sits at a table, holding a list of taxes owed by citizens. A second official records the tax payment, and the third holds a balance scale to verify the weight of gold coins. Like the boxed Roman weights-and-scale set from the fourth-century, housed at the Petrie Museum in London, the balance represented a religion-based government. The Petrie's set contains four flat weights with a cross framed by a wreath on each one.

We can still purchase balance scales today, for business or as novelties. This scale also remains a symbol of today's legal system. The Scales of Justice—held by Lady Justice wrapped in flowing robes and sometimes wearing a blindfold—measure the strength of a case's support or opposition.

In other early trade transactions, some stoppers used to cap *amphorae* (pottery storage jars), sported Christian crosses. So did the stamps on the neck, side or handles of these shapely vessels, and the lead *bullae* (seals) that closed other containers. Crosses designated quality products within. A fourth- to fifth-century *amphora* lifted from a Black Sea shipwreck carries a stamp actually in the shape of a Latin cross. An inscription on the cross reads, "Mother of God Help this Deed [of mine]." In this case, the stamp served as a guarantee of quality and a plea for assistance.

Trusting the Promise

We, too, want to trust the reliability of the Christian cross's promise to us. The writer of a letter to Timothy assured believers with these personal facts: "Here is a trustworthy saying that deserves full acceptance: Christ Jesus came into the world to save sinners—of whom I am the worst. But for that very reason I was shown mercy so that in me, the worst of sinners, Christ Jesus might display his unlimited patience as an example for those who would believe on him and receive eternal life" (1 Tim 1:15-16).

Like these early Christians, the weight of our convictions shape into the cross. It is our trustworthy standard. But today, how does the cross appear to those outside the faith? Can they trust it? Think of a Nazi-era Jew, a Rwandan refugee, an alternative lifestyle American? Does the cross represent safety, quality, loving care, reliability? Does it draw or repel? Punish or heal? These are troubling questions, worth our attention.

On the other hand, these questions represent far-reaching issues that can't be solved easily or quickly. But in our daily lives, we could more carefully represent the cross. We could extend what we receive from Christ and his cross—patience, compassion, forgiveness, acceptance—to the people we live with and meet. We could become their trustworthy standard.

26

Coins for the Kingdom

Now have come the salvation and the power and the kingdom of our God, and the authority of his Christ. —REVELATION 12:10

**A Constantine Coin
with Christogram**

THROUGHOUT HUMAN HISTORY, money has changed people and things. But people and things have also changed money, especially when a new Roman emperor ascended the throne. It's possible to trace the lineage of Roman emperors and their beliefs by sorting through the images and inscriptions on the empire's coins. Emperor egos couldn't resist expressing power and authority via monetary exchange, a system that almost everyone under their rule participated in. Even John Chrysostom, a fourth-century spiritual leader in favor of strict asceticism, observed, "The use of coins welds together our whole life, and is the basis of all our transactions. Whenever anything is to be bought or sold, we do it all through coins."

Constantine's ego was no exception, and he continued the imperial tradition of ubiquity by gracing coins with his image. The British Mu-

seum in London claims, "One important legacy of Constantine's authority is his coinage. The coins of Constantine and his sons are still
some of the most common to be dug up in Britain today." Three coins
displayed at this museum exemplify Constantine's influence on coinage, gradually replacing pagan images with Christian symbolism and
in particular, the cross.

A silver coin from the beginning of Constantine's reign (c. AD 306-
307) depicts the profile of a young man wearing the Roman laurel
leaf. Created when Constantine still held the title of Caesar, the reverse side of the coin features the gate of a Roman military camp. The
museum titles the coin's description "A Symbol of Security," emphasizing the empire's military might.

After Constantine became the sole Roman emperor, in the early
fourth century he distributed a golden coin with his profile looking
heavenward. Although some images of Alexander the Great (336-323
BC) exhibited this pose, the museum explains that Constantine's upward look suggests his dependence on God and titles its display "Divine Inspiration." In contrast, the back of the coin illustrates Constantine's brutality toward his enemies. Although ancient Romans wouldn't
think of this two-sided coin as thematically inconsistent, today we'd
criticize Constantine for his mixed messages.

Eventually the coins for the Roman empire featured small images of the Christogram, an image of the Chi-Rho cross he saw in
the sky before his battle at Milvian Bridge in AD 312. A third coin
at the British Museum, minted in the mid-fourth century, displays
a Christogram on its reverse side. The museum displays this coin
with the title "The First Symbol of Christian Faith." The museum
explains, "The example illustrated shows the Christogram in its
fullest form. . . . Though the western provinces of the Roman
Empire were Latin-speaking, and the Greek letters would have
been meaningless to most people, the symbolism would have been
instantly recognized."

Roman Coins with the Cross

Even though Constantine introduced Christian images, he still circulated coins that joined his image with pagan symbols like the sun god, especially at the beginning of his reign. This religious syncretism decorated the empire's coins until Emperor Theodosius declared Christianity the empire's official religion in the late fourth century. While emperors still graced the coinage, increasingly the cross appeared with the rulers and pagan images disappeared.

By the reign of Theodosius II in the fifth century, coins adopted an "overtly Christian character." Over time, the cross supplanted long-standing pagan themes on the coins. For example, the female Victory image began holding a cross instead of a staff, and eventually she turned into the archangel Michael shouldering a cross and a *globus crucige* (an orb topped by a cross). The orb-and-cross images represented the emperor's divine authority. A popular seventh-century motif on Byzantine coins displayed the cross at the top of three stairs, commemorating Christ's journey to Golgotha. With the exception of a century of iconoclasm, when Christians debated the use of sacred images, Byzantine rulers imprinted coins with crosses until the fifteenth century. As the golden money changed hands, Roman citizens exchanged these small crosses, the symbols of a higher and lasting authority.

Our Own Uncertain Times

In our own uncertain times, Roman "cross coins" speak to us about the true source of security. Ultimately, we can't depend on coins or paper money or employment or prosperity to provide daily necessities or secure the future. History warns that mighty kingdoms like the Roman Empire eventually fall. The Visigoths destroyed the Western empire when they sacked Rome in 410 and carried away prisoners, including the emperor's sister. After a struggling revival the Eastern empire fell a second and final time in 1453 when Ottoman Turks captured Constantinople.

Ironically, cross-imprinted coins from these governments have survived, directing us to Christ. He urges us to ask for our daily bread; to not think about tomorrow; to not lay up treasures in heaven. Instead, he'll provide for us. I crave the simplicity of the Lord's directives, but it's hard to *truly believe* and follow them when money dwindles and bills pile up. I keep thinking if I earn more money I'd be secure, not considering that banks fail, stock markets plummet and cash loses its value.

When economies falter, we're led back to Christ's words. His promise of provision transcends the transition of world leaders, the pillage of empires and the collapse of economies. He assures us: in God we can trust.

PART SIX

Ways to Worship

The Cross in Early Church Life

Now that we have seen the resurrection of Christ, let us adore the all-holy Lord Jesus, the only sinless one. We bow in worship before your cross, O Christ, and we praise and glorify your resurrection, for you are our God, and we have no other, and we magnify your name. All you faithful, come: let us adore the holy resurrection of Christ, for, behold, through the cross joy has come to the world! Let us always bless the Lord, let us sing his resurrection, for by enduring for us the pain of the cross, he has crushed death by his death.

EASTER SUNDAY PROCLAMATION,
ORTHODOX LITURGY

27

Walking the Cross

Whoever claims to live in him must walk as Jesus did. —1 JOHN 2:6

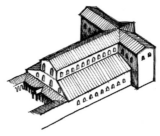

A Cross-Shaped Basilica Plan

As a young girl, I heard that early Christians devoted themselves to fellowship, breaking bread and moving from house to house for teachings. I envisioned a rollicking, undisciplined group—a sort of progressive-meal praise party, where spontaneity ruled for years. So when I eventually learned the early church first worshiped in synagogues, then in home services, and developed its own liturgy, my imagination back-stepped. The early church, in style and structure, was more orderly than I'd thought.

By the early fourth century Christians worshiped in halls, but in the earlier years they'd gathered in private rooms or house-churches. According to custom, late antiquity Romans adorned their homes with images, but to date only one example of a decorated house church exists. In the 1920s and 1930s, excavators unearthed a typical court-yard house in Dura Europas, a prosperous trading post in Syria. Dated before AD 256, the owners had converted their house into a place of worship, complete with a baptistery and wall images of the Good Shepherd and scenes from Christ's life. Though modest, the Dura home foretold the vast, symbolic churches of the future.

Walking Around the Cross

After Constantine officially accepted Christianity in AD 313, believers emerged from house churches and worshiped publicly. The emperor embarked on an ambitious church-building program, mostly in Rome but also in other populated regions in the empire. One art historian explains:

> The modest buildings and houses adequate for the simple early Christian service became inappropriate once Constantine recognized Christianity as one of the state religions. . . . The ever-present symbolic focus of Christianity demanded that the Church signify both the house of God and the tomb of Christ. The building had to be majestic, worthy of the Ruler of Heaven. Furthermore, this heavenly mansion had to house the entire Christian community.

To meet these requirements, architects modeled the first "official" churches after a structure they knew well: the Roman basilica, a rectangular administrative building located in a city forum or marketplace. The basilica's long, roomy interior space and good lighting from high windows adapted well to large groups of people. Flanked by rows of columns forming aisles on each side, visitors walked the basilica's length to reach the apse, a rounded extension used as a law court. Often builders constructed an apse on each end of the building to accommodate multiple proceedings. Visitors entered the basilica through its many side doors, and looking up, a timber truss roof contrasted with the building's massive masonry construction.

When architects adapted the basilica plan into a church building, they created more room for congregants and assigned new, spiritual meaning to spaces within the structure. Adapted for a pilgrim church like Old Saint Peter's basilica in Rome, completed in AD 329 but later destroyed by fire, visitors first walked through an atrium that led to a portal (doorway). After entering the narthex (vestibule), pilgrims stepped down the vertical nave, leading to the apse, the niche that held the memorial to Peter, the "rock" on whom Christ built his church. However, before reaching the apse visitors crossed a transept, a space that intersected the nave with an aisle projecting to the right and left. Symbolically, this horizontal aisle formed the crossbeam of a cross. As architects innovated on this design for churches, mausoleums and monasteries, they enlarged the area behind the apse, which housed the altar, and the cross shape grew more distinct. Anyone walking the length and width of a sanctuary's aisles traced the cross.

Other notable early churches built from the basilica plan in the fourth and fifth centuries included the Church of Saint John Lateran in Rome (318); the Church of the Nativity in Bethlehem (c. 333); the Church of the Holy Sepulcher in Jerusalem (335); the Church of Santa Sabina in Rome (c. 422-432); and Saint Maria Maggiore in Rome (432-440). Along with Old Saint Peter's, these churches set a pattern for traditional, Western church buildings ever since.

Hospitality of the Heart

I often joke that I initially worshiped in a liturgical church because I loved the building. Actually, it's true. The stone chapel, built in the cross or cruciform style, combined the best of Romanesque and Gothic architecture. As I walked toward the church's west entrance, a gargoyle stared down at me, usually scolding me for being late. Within moments, though, I discarded his condescension when the sculptured portal ushered me inside, into a quieting ritual before worship. As I stood in the narthex, my brain and body hushed while my eyes adjusted to the semi-darkness. Then I clattered along the nave to locate a seat, identifying the noisy tile floors as the only decorative feature I didn't like.

During the service I stared at the sturdy columns attached to high arches, the carved altar and lectern, and the stained-glass windows. Participating in communion, I walked up the nave, across the right transept, down a side aisle, across the back aisle and up the nave again to recapture my place on a pew. But I didn't realize I'd just traced the right side of a cross. However, with time I learned it wasn't just the architectural features that drew me into this chapel. The symbolism of "walking the cross" stirred my spirit. I thought about what the cross meant to my faith, my life. I considered Jesus, who "walked the cross" long before me.

In a cross-shaped church, to worship means following the way of Christ. The twentieth-century German priest and academic, Romano Guardini, extolled the sacred character of a cruciform church and its influence.

> It is the doors that admit us to this mysterious place. Lay aside, they say, all that cramps and narrows, all that sinks the mind. Open your heart, lift up your eyes. Let your soul be free, for this is God's temple.
>
> It is likewise the representation of you, yourself. For you, your soul and your body, are the living temple of God. Open up that temple, make it spacious, give it light. . . . Of small use to you is a house of wood and stone unless you yourself are God's living dwelling. The high arched gates may be lifted up, and the portals parted wide, but unless the doors of your heart are open, how can the King of Glory enter in?

If we're attentive, walking the length and width of a cross-shaped church identifies us with Christ—and measures the hospitality of our hearts.

28

Follow Me

*To this you were called, because Christ suffered for you, leaving you
an example, that you should follow in his steps.* —1 PETER 2:21

**The Dumbarton Oaks
Syrian Processional Cross**

I RARELY SING THE OPENING or closing hymns during a liturgical
service. I'm captivated by the solemn processional and recessional that
begins and ends a liturgy. Instead of singing, I watch the slowly moving verger, acolytes, choir members, readers, deacons, clergy and others who guide the worship. The organ music, the candles, the vestments, the gospel book carried facing forward and the processional
cross held high enhance the pageantry. These processions connect me
to congregations of ages past, to the millions of Christians who've
participated in the rituals and observances of the universal church.
Few liturgical objects from the earliest church have survived, but the
ceremonies still thrive.

Early Roman church ordines (books with instructions for liturgical
functions) indicate that a cross led sacred Christian processions dur-

ing the Middle Ages, and every church owned one. Carried primarily during services, the processional cross was mounted on a pole and detachable. With the exception of a papal pageant, a cross or a crucifix faced the direction of the procession, with church leaders and congregants walking behind it, affirming their role as Christ's followers. When not in use, the cross stood in an upright base by the altar. Processional crosses also led imperial processions, military campaigns, sacred festivals and visits to sacred sites.

A hymn in honor of the cross, composed in the sixth century, contains one of the earliest references to the processional cross. However, it's possible this ceremonial cross existed even earlier. Before the age of Constantine, Christians walked in solemn funeral processions, and in the second century Tertullian of Carthage, a church father, referred to formal progressions related to church services. By the seventh century in Rome, the cross played a role in papal processions at the request of Pope Gregory the Great. Byzantines also created processional crosses for their ceremonies.

Cross Gifts and Elaborations

As Christianity spread, processional crosses from both the West and East ranged from simple metalwork to elaborate bejeweled treasures, depending on the wealth of a congregation or prestige of a religious leader. Images on the crosses often drew from biblical sources and inscriptions varied widely, including references to whomever owned or donated it as a gift. For example, the Dumbarton Oaks Research Library in Washington, D.C., displays a sixth-century bronze processional cross discovered in Syria. Small engravings on the cross include Jesus holding a book and raising his hand in blessings, Mary with arms uplifted in worship and two angels in flight. The inscription reads, "For the forgiveness of the sins of Leontia."

In the tenth century the Visigoth King Pelayo believed the simple wooden cross he carried into battle ensured his victory over the

Arabs. This Cross of Victory, now in the Oviedo Cathedral in northern Spain, became a symbol of the *Reconquista* and metalworkers covered it with gold and densely placed precious stones.

The twelfth-century Cross of Cong, a processional cross commissioned by the King of Ireland, echoes the best of eighth-century Celtic metalwork. Artisans covered the oak base with gold, silver, niello, copper, bronze, brass, enamel, precious stones, colored glass, rock crystal, filigree work, spirals and animals. The cross, now kept by the National Museum in Dublin, also served as a reliquary for the True Cross. The Latin inscription on the cross reads, "In this cross is covered the cross on which the Founder of the world suffered."

Many simple processional crosses humbly served the Christian world's small parishes. But with royalty and the religious elite commissioning costly crosses, the meaning of a church processional could blur. Who did the processional represent? Who were the clergy and the congregants actually following? Based on its original meaning, the processional cross implored them to follow Christ.

It still calls to us today.

The Perilous Call to Follow

It's no secret that before Augustine of Hippo's conversion to Christianity, he lived raucously in the pagan milieu of the fourth century. From the example of Monica his mother, Augustine knew what following Christ looked like, but he couldn't paint that picture for himself. In his book *Confessions,* Augustine recounted the sins of his youth and how his prayers rang with insincerity. "Give me chastity and continence," he told God, "but not yet." Eventually, Augustine altered his prayer, transforming into a Latin church father, the bishop of Hippo, and an influential theologian.

We can identify with Augustine's earlier indecision, though. Standing at the crossroads between the way of Christ and the way of self-gratification, the inspirational pageantry of the processional cross looks nowhere in sight. We only hear the quiet voice calling, "Follow me" (Mt 4:19). But how do we follow?

Clement of Rome explained that we follow Christ if "our understanding is fixed by faith towards God. If we earnestly seek the things that are pleasing and acceptable to Him. If we do the things that are in harmony with His blameless will. And if we follow the way of truth, casting away from us all unrighteousness." The first-century bishop's words sound simple enough, but the journey isn't easy. Jesus leads up down a narrow, solitary, hazardous footpath, a path I slide off easily.

Two thousand years later, every Christian I know struggles to follow Clement's seemingly simple instructions. However, if I think of the roadway as a relationship, and not a set of rules, I stress less. The twentieth-century theologian, Dietrich Bonhoeffer, lends insight to this attitude toward the journey:

> If we follow this way as one we follow in obedience to an external command, if we are afraid of ourselves all the time, it is indeed an impossible way. But if we behold Jesus Christ going on before us step by step, we shall not go astray. If we worry about the dangers that beset us, if we gaze at the road instead of at him who goes before, we are already straying from the path. For he is himself the way, the narrow way, and the strait gate. He, and he alone, is our journey's end.

From beginning to end, following the cross leads us to Christ.

29

The Cross and the Water

[You have been] been buried with him in baptism and
raised with him through your faith in the power of God,
who raised him from the dead. —COLOSSIANS 2:12

The Rock Baptismal Font at Shivta

In CHRISTIANITY, ALL ROADS LEAD to the cross. Whatever the be-lief, whatever the sacrament, it can't be fully understood without Christ's sacrificial death. Ancient baptismal fonts often expressed this symbolism: they formed a cross, symbolizing the Lord's burial and resurrection. Some of the oldest cross fonts excavated by archaeolo-gists were rock-hewn in Israel, such as the fourth-century baptismal font from the northern church in Shivta, and the font from the sixth-century central church at Lower Herodium. These fonts, each carved from a single stone, cleansed repentant sinners with the waters of new life.

Although baptism focused on water, to engage this sacrament's full meaning, Christians also acknowledged the life-changing cross. In Tertullian of Carthage's treatise on baptism, written at

**The rock baptismal font from the Northern Church. Shivta, Israel.
Fourth century.**

the beginning of the third century, he associated baptismal water
with the cross. After extolling the significance of water in Christ's
ministry, the church father wrote, "Onward he presses, to the
passion—and it too witnesses [the water] of baptism. For as he
surrenders to the cross, water again intervenes—witness the
washing of Pilate's hands; witness the wound in his side, where
water gushes out; witness the soldier's lance!" Baptism and crucifixion served as bookends to Christ's ministry, yet the sanctifying
water couldn't exist without the bloody cross. The ancient church
revered this water-to-wood connection, and solemn preparations
preceded baptism.

Although the first Christians waded into water soon after they
accepted Christ, in the next centuries adult baptism required an
intense preparation, including prayer, teaching, repentance, exorcism, fasting and other rituals. By the fourth century, this
preparation divided into four parts. It included the inquirer stage,
when clergy investigated whether someone could enter the preparation process; the catechumen stage, when Christians received

instruction in doctrine and holy living; the enlightenment stage, when the catechumens entered a strict preparation for baptism; and the baptism, welcoming a believer into the full life of the church on *Pascha* (Easter). After baptism, Christians called themselves "the faithful."

During the enlightenment stage, catechumens faced a formal interrogation, "followed by the making of the sign of the cross on the forehead, an initial exorcism of evil spirits, the imposition of hands by the bishop, and the eating of a tiny bit of salt." The salt symbolized wisdom, good works and freedom from sin.

The pilgrim Egeria visited Jerusalem in the fourth century and described the questioning process:

> Names must be given in before the first day of Lent, which lasts eight weeks here. . . . When the priest has taken down all the names the bishop's chair is placed in the middle of the Great Church. The priests sit in chairs on either side of him and the other clergy stand nearby. One by one the candidates for baptism are led forward, men coming with their godfathers and women with their godmothers. As they come in one by one the bishop asks their neighbors questions about them: Is this person leading a good life? Does he respect his parents? Is he a drunkard or a boaster? If the candidate proves to be without fault in these matters the bishop writes down his name; but if someone is accused of anything, he is asked to leave and told: "Amend your life and when that is done approach the baptismal font."

At the Baptismal Font

After catechumens passed the intense moral questioning, they prepared for baptism, an act indicating their spiritual rebirth and enlightenment. At the fourth-century Church of Moses on Mount Nebo in Jordan, an inscription called its baptismal font the "holy pool of rebirth." Stonecutters shaped the pool into a cross. When workers rebuilt the baptismal in the late sixth century, they inscribed the baptistery chapel floor with these words: "The place where people are enlightened."

Clement of Alexandria explained this enlightenment:

> When we are baptized, we are enlightened. Being enlightened, we are adopted as sons. Adopted as sons, we are made perfect. Made perfect, we become immortal . . . "and sons all of the Most High" [Ps. 82:6]. This work is variously called grace, illumination, perfection, and washing. It is a washing by which we are cleansed of sins; a gift of grace by which the punishments due our sins are remitted; an illumination by which we behold that holy light of salvation—that is, by which we see God clearly; and we call that perfection which leaves nothing lacking.

Celebrating the Sacred Water

Baptism also instigated a communal celebration. For example, in the fifth century at the Byzantine Basilica of Saint Theodore of Gerasa, also in Jordan, two rooms connected by a corridor formed a baptismal complex. The corridor attached a chapel to the side of the church. Much like other catechumens in other locations, in the southern room a candidate for baptism abandoned his or her clothes, received a full-body anointing in *chism* (holy oil), and descended into a cross-shaped pool for baptism by a bishop, priest, deacon or deaconess. (Men and women were separated for baptism, with deaconesses tending to the women.) The baptized Christian then entered the adjoining room, donned a white garment and proceeded to the chapel to celebrate a first Eucharist. During this service, the freshly baptized drank a cup of milk and honey, symbolizing the Lord's nurturing presence for his "newborns." He or she also wore the white garment for seven more days.

Appropriately, the cross-shaped fonts of early Christianity immersed believers into the rituals and mysteries of baptism. They stepped out of the water enlightened, committed and released into new life. An anonymous epistle widely read by first-century Christians claimed, "Blessed are they who, placing their trust in the cross, have gone down into the water."

In the same manner, when we approach the baptismal font, we can remember the cross. We can contemplate the sacred water and remember we are blessed.

30

Breaking the Bread

While they were eating, Jesus took bread, gave thanks
and broke it, and gave it to his disciples, saying,
"Take and eat; this is my body." —MATTHEW 26:26

A Bread Stamp with a Cross

DEEP IN THE RUINS OF POMPEII, covered by volcanic ash in the first century, archaeologists unearthed the remains of public bakeries. Historians believe these bakeries with their huge ovens not only supplied bread for Pompeii, but also surrounding towns. Throughout the Roman Empire, only the rich could afford ovens, so many people carted grain to the bakeries for grinding and making bread. In turn, laws required bakers to stamp their bread dough with a distinctive design to trace the sources of loaves. This helped to ensure quality and prevent theft, especially of imperial supplies.

However, with the advent of Christianity, these applied-by-hand bread stamps acquired new meaning. Christians donated bread to the church and the stone or pottery stamps distinguished between loaves used for the Eucharist and those blessed and distributed to pilgrims and congregants. Stamps for Eucharist bread often bore the symbol of the cross and indicated where the priest should tear the loaf, releasing Christ's body to partakers in this sacrament. Of all the im-

Bread stamps with crosses. Israel Museum, Jerusalem. Byzantine period.

ages that could be stamped on a loaf of communion bread, the cross was the most fitting. It bore the body of Christ, broken for humanity.

Jesus and a Hungry World

During his ministry Jesus often spoke about bread. He was born in Bethlehem, which means "house of bread," when Roman citizens began to hunger. The ruling caste hadn't yet perceived the growing lack of bread—the empire's chief food staple—but agrarians in the provinces heard their own stomachs growling. "Therefore, the people asked one question of each new prophet: Was he concerned about the price of bread? And did he have food for them?"

Perhaps in an act of solidarity with the hungry laboring class, Jesus prepared for ministry by fasting for forty days. At the height of his hunger, the devil tempted him to transform stones into bread. Jesus replied by quoting ancient Hebrew Scripture: "It is written: 'Man does not live on bread alone, but on every word that comes from the mouth of God'" (Mt 4:4; Deut 8:3). Since the beginning of time, humans had overlooked feeding their souls.

However, relief workers say starving people need tangible, satiating food before they can focus on much else. No doubt, Jesus knew this.

When he taught his followers to pray, he included, "Give us this day our daily bread" (Mt 6:11) and one of his most famous miracles was practical. He fed a hungry crowd of five thousand with five bread loaves and two fish. A day later, Jesus parlayed this remarkable meal into a spiritual lesson. "I tell you the truth, you are looking for me, not because you saw miraculous signs but because you ate the loaves and had your fill," he began. "Do not work for food that spoils, but for food that endures to eternal life, which the Son of Man will give you. On him God the Father has placed his seal of approval" (Jn 6:26-27). Like an emblem on a bread loaf, Jesus bore the Ruler's approval for feeding the spiritually hungry.

When Jews grumbled about these claims, Jesus directly compared himself to bread and alluded to the cross. He explained, "I am the living bread that came down from heaven. If anyone eats of this bread, he will live forever. This bread is my flesh, which I will give for the life of the world" (Jn 6:51). When Jesus clarified that people must eat his flesh and drink his blood to gain life, the metaphor stumped his followers. "This is a hard teaching," they complained. "Who can accept it?" (Jn 6:60). Many quit following the Teacher and wandered back home. But Jesus set his eyes on Golgotha. To save a hungering world, the bread needed the stamp of the cross.

As Jesus neared his appointed death, he taught the disciples more about the bread-cross connection. At the Passover meal with his disciples, "he took bread, gave thanks and broke it, and gave it to them, saying, 'This is my body given for you; do this in remembrance of me'" (Lk 22:19). Soon Jesus would be the torn-apart bread, broken for the world's spiritual hunger.

Bread and the Holy Eucharist

Soon after the descent of the Holy Spirit and before the New Testament writings, Christians broke bread together in remembrance of Christ. This practice began humbly in homes, accompanied by spontaneous hymns and prayers. In the next few centuries church leaders developed liturgies to accompany this bread-and-wine remembrance, the Eucharist. Early liturgies from the first through the fourth centuries have been attributed to James the brother of Christ; Mark the disciple of Peter the apostle; Pope Clement I of Rome; Basil the Great, Bishop of Caesarea; John Chrysostom, Bishop of Constantinople and others. In the second century the apologist Justin Martyr recorded the earliest known description of a Eucharist service, celebrated on the first day of the week. The celebration incorporated Scripture reading, an exhortation, various prayers, the offering of bread, wine and water, thanksgiving, partaking of Holy Communion, and a collection for charity.

In the Divine Liturgy by John Chrysostom, before congregants received the bread, the priest recalled the crucifixion and resurrection. He recited, "Having beheld the resurrection of Christ, let us worship the holy Lord Jesus, the only Sinless One. We venerate Your cross, O Christ, and we praise and glorify Your holy resurrection. . . . For behold, through the cross joy has come to all the world. Blessing the Lord always, let us praise His resurrection. For enduring the cross for us, He destroyed death by death." In this ancient liturgy, the bread pointed to the cross.

However early Christians celebrated the Eucharist, they also remembered words from the apostle Paul. He'd reminded the primitive church that celebrating the Lord's Supper—eating the bread and drinking the wine—proclaimed Christ's death on the cross (1 Cor 11:26). Jesus was the bread, broken for them. He is the one broken for us.

31

Take This Cup

Is not the cup of thanksgiving for which we give thanks a
participation in the blood of Christ? —1 CORINTHIANS 10:16

Syrian Chalice with
Apostles Venerating the Cross

JESUS DIDN'T EVADE talking about blood.

At the Last Supper the Lord foretold his death on the cross. He raised
a cup of wine and memorialized these words: "Drink from it, all of you.
This is my blood of the covenant, which is poured out for many for the
forgiveness of sins" (Mt 26:27-28). The Jewish-born disciples understood animal sacrifice for the forgiveness of sins. But drinking Christ's
blood? This could have prompted questions and queasiness.

Blood makes us uneasy. It's messy and portends injury, suffering
and death. We divert ourselves from staring at it, thinking about it,
especially if the blood profuses freely. Judging by some early Christian
and medieval artifacts, this could be how we—the historical church—
sometimes handled Christ's blood. We overlooked it and obsessed
about the cup. The cup could be exciting. The cup could be stunning.

The cup could be prestigious. It was easier to concentrate on the cup. We spent ambitious amounts of time on forming, decorating and revering the communion cup.

Medieval romance writers bypassed Christ's blood and told mystical stories about his cup, naming it the Holy Grail. In turn, believers and adventurers have plumbed the Grail's mysteries for centuries, even claiming it was really a woman—the faithful Mary Magdalene—instead of a drinking vessel. Finally, in the early twentieth century researchers found a plain silver chalice (drinking cup), in Antioch, Syria, and ambitiously identified it as Christ's cup, dating it to the first century. They presumed that within a century after Christ's death, silversmiths had designed the elaborate encasing around the plain cup. Birds, animals and grapevines inhabit the gilded shell, along with twelve male figures seated in chairs, ambiguously identified as the apostles or classical philosophers. Some experts believe two of the figures represent Christ.

In 1933 the World's Fair displayed the chalice as "the Holy Grail," but since then scholars refuted that claim. Instead, the Antioch Chalice probably dates to the early sixth century, used as a cup for serving the Eucharist in or near Antioch. For explorers, this identification left the possibility that Christ's cup still exists somewhere.

The Treasure in a Chalice

If we weren't questing for the cup, we were decorating it. Granted, the ancient Eucharist chalices on view today survived wars and the Reformation because of their value. People from diverse eras and locations considered these vessels worth saving and kept them protected. Simple parish cups must have outnumbered the ornate chalices created for the wealthy, but liturgical objects gathering the most attention in art exhibits tend toward the exceptional.

Noteworthy Eucharist cups created before the first millennium can be found in museums around the world. For example, attributed to both the second or first century BC and the twelfth century AD, the

Chalice of the Abbot Suger of Saint-Denis Abbey in France now belongs to the National Gallery of Art in the United States. The museum describes it as "one of the most splendid treasures from the Middle Ages." Suger's goldsmiths created a mount for the cup, originally carved from sardonyx in Alexandria, Egypt before Christ's time. The final chalice exhibited gold, silver, filigree, gems, a medallion of Christ and the inscription Greek, "I am the Alpha and Omega, the Beginning and the End." This and other Eucharist cups displayed the finest metalworking from their time.

Amazingly, some of the most famous chalices do not prominently display the cross or anything related to the crucifixion. They're beautiful but devoid of references to the blood they signified during a Eucharist service. However, a lesser-known chalice in Baltimore's Walters Art Museum meets this expectation and honors the cross. Discovered with twenty-three altar vessels in Syria, the silver, arcaded "Chalice with Apostles Venerating the Cross" highlights two pairs of apostles alternated with large crosses. Byzantine Christians probably hid the chalice and other liturgical vessels when Arabs invaded their land. The Greek inscription reads: "Treasure of St. Sergios of the village of Kaper Koraon."

Materially, many ancient Eucharist chalices qualified as treasures. Accomplished artisans meticulously chose the finest metals and jewels, techniques and creativity, to make them. However, the most valued treasure by far settled within the cup: the blood of Christ, spilled on the cross and poured out in remembrance of him. "This cup is the new covenant in my blood; do this, whenever you drink it, in remembrance of me" he said at the Last Supper. "For whenever you . . . drink this cup, you proclaim the Lord's death until he comes" (1 Cor 11:25-26).

Drinking from the Cup

The Lord's lifted cup turned the disciples toward the cross. When his friends drank from this chalice, they agreed to partake of his bloody suffering. This cup demanded so much, not even Jesus wanted to drink it. Scripture records the Lord's reluctance:

> Then Jesus went with his disciples to a place called Gethsemane, and he said to them, "Sit here while I go over there and pray." He took Peter and the two sons of Zebedee along with him, and he began to be sorrowful and troubled. Then he said to them, "My soul is overwhelmed with sorrow to the point of death. Stay here and keep watch with me."
>
> Going a little farther, he fell with his face to the ground and prayed, "My Father, if it is possible, may this cup be taken from me. Yet not as I will, but as you will."
>
> "Then he returned to his disciples and found them sleeping. 'Could you men not keep watch with me for one hour?" he asked Peter. "Watch and pray so that you will not fall into temptation. The spirit is willing, but the body is weak."
>
> He went away a second time and prayed, "My Father, if it is not possible for this cup to be taken away unless I drink it, may your will be done."
>
> When he came back, he again found them sleeping, because their eyes were heavy. So he left them and went away once more and prayed the third time, saying the same thing. (Mt 26:36-43)

When soldiers arrived, Jesus accepted the cup, doing his father's will.

Christ asks us, along with the disciples, "Can you drink the cup I am going to drink?" (Mt 20:22). Will we do God's will? With the simplest communion chalice, we answer him.

32

Decorating the Sacred

One thing I ask of the LORD, this is what I seek: that I may dwell in the house of the LORD all the days of my life, to gaze upon the beauty of the LORD and to seek him in his temple. —PSALM 27:4

A Sion Treasure Polycandelon

Entering the Byzantine church at nightfall, worshipers paused, adjusting their eyes to the dimness. Stirred by gusts in the doorway or human movement, hanging polycandela (oil lamps) gently swayed, casting shadowy crosses on the floor. Suspended by chains and holding small cups of burning oil, the cross-shaped ornaments summoned "otherworldliness." In the sparse yet sacred light, early Christians reflected on matters of the spirit.

These light sources, crafted in silver and niello (incised designs), belonged to the Sion Treasure later unearthed in Southern Turkey during the 1960s. A church or monastery, probably named "Holy Sion," owned this magnificent group of sixth-century liturgical objects and church furnishings. At least twelve polycandela belonged to the treasure, along with wine chalices, large patens (plates) for Eucharist bread, a peacock censer (incense burner), oil lamps, crosses, book covers and other silver items. Most of the Sion Treasure's seventy-one high-quality objects surfaced in excellent condition, except for a few bent or crushed articles. The damaged pieces suggested that Byzantine imperial authorities wanted to melt down the liturgical silver to pay wages for the emperor's army during enemy invasions. Evidently, clergy thought sacred objects deserved a burial instead of surviving as common coins.

Although divided into separate exhibitions, the Sion Treasure objects still project an overall reverence for the cross. The cross decorates many objects, but the patens that held the flat, unleavened bread reveal the style of this community's worship. The center of two patens at Dumbarton Oaks feature an engraved cross, and a third, larger and elaborately decorated plate carries a Christogram. Artisans formed this paten's broad rim in repoussé (a raised surface), and Dumbarton Oaks describes the result as "a multilayered surface that is highly animated by reflections of light, a variety of textures, and the application of gilding."

This paten and the entire collection demonstrate Byzantium's regard for churches and their décor. Christians wanted the finest for the Lord's house. God deserved quality. However, quality didn't just dwell with the wealthy or privileged or Byzantine. Smaller churches with limited resources in other locations offered the best they could afford for worship.

Beauty in the Real and Obscure

With the overwhelming attention drawn to mosaics and carvings, relics and paintings, we can miss the equally beautiful but smaller aspects of early church decoration. Magnificent buildings like Hagia Sophia in Istanbul, Turkey, and the mosaics of San Vitale and other churches in Ravenna, Italy, overshadow the hardworking liturgical vessels and practical furnishings for ancient worship services. Books and websites about art and architecture usually prefer the glittering cross of Emperor Justinian II from imperial Constantinople versus the terracotta bowl of a forgotten desert congregation.

However, the humble artifacts teach us about real-world worship of the past. A stone chancel fragment. A cracked, marble-but-modest altar. A scarred spoon for serving mixed bread and wine. A hanging bronze censer or etched glass bowl. Encountering these—all bearing an image of the cross—enlighten us to the sacred, recurring, universal rituals of the early church. A group of bronze crosses attached by chains and hung from ceiling beams indicates that everyday citizens valued the cross for more than pomp and circumstance. These crosses participated in the sanctity of simple worship.

The apostle Paul compared Christians to these functional remnants, identifying our true treasure. He assured them, "[God] made his light shine in our hearts to give us the light of the knowledge of the glory of God in the face of Christ. But we have this treasure in jars of clay to show that this all-surpassing power is from God and not from us" (2 Cor 4:6-7). To showcase God's power, Christ used pottery rather than precious metal, the practical over the spectacular.

In our culture of shock and awe, it's not clever or memorable to emulate Christ and choose the ordinary. On the other hand, our ordinariness might be what best communicates the cross's ability to transform us. More power inhabits an honest, satisfied spiritual life than owning the world's greatest treasures.

In the fourth century, Augustine of Hippo wanted to exchange these treasures for the "treasures of wisdom and knowledge." He modeled how we can prefer righteousness over riches:

> We ask not of you, O Father, silver and gold, honor and glory, nor the pleasures of the world, but grant us grace to seek your kingdom and your righteousness, and add to us things necessary

for the body and for this life. Behold, O Lord, our desire: may it be pleasing in your sight.

 We present our petition to you through our Lord Jesus Christ, who is at our right hand, our mediator and advocate, through whom you sought us that we might seek you; your Word, though whom you made us and all things; your only begotten Son, through whom you called us to adoption, who intercedes with you for us, and in whom are hid all the treasures of wisdom and knowledge; to him, with yourself and the Holy Spirit, be all honor, praise, and glory, now and forever. Amen.

33

The Iconoclastic Cross

[Christ's] purpose was to create in himself one new man out
of the two, thus making peace, and in this one body to
reconcile both of them to God through the cross, by which
he put to death their hostility. —EPHESIANS 2:15-16

Crucifixion in the
Khludov Psalter

IN THE SEVENTH CENTURY a Christian woman who adored the martyrs and healers, Cosmas and Damian, painted illustrations of them on the inside walls of her house. When the woman later fell terribly ill, she crawled out of bed. With her fingernails, she scraped plaster from the images, stirred the particles in water, and drank the mixture. Supposedly, it cured her immediately.

It's an extreme story—and most likely a legend—that illustrates the early Byzantine belief that sacred images could perform miracles. Although artists probably didn't initially create religious artwork with this idea in mind, the misguided conviction about images spread through the empire. This approach to sacred images eventually provoked a clash of opinion in the eighth and ninth centuries. However, the issue was more fundamental than miracles. Christians asked, "Is it biblical to create sacred images at all?" That's not a question bothering us much today, but in Byzantium, it created a furor based on the Second Commandment.

God and Graven Images

According to Scripture, God dictated the Ten Commandments to Moses on Mount Sinai, along with other laws for the Israelite nation. The Second Commandment addressed the issue of idolatry and creating images to worship. It said, "Thou shalt not make unto thee any graven image, or any likeness of any thing that is in heaven above, or that is in the earth beneath, or that is in the water under the earth" (Ex 20:4 KJV).

This was serious business for the Israelites. The Second Commandment was the only law in the Decalogue (Commandments) accompanied by the promise of a generational curse or blessing (Ex 5-6). It also distinguished the Israelites from—even pitted them against—surrounding cultures that crafted pagan idols from wood, stone and precious metals. Various Jewish legal codes also stated this no-graven-image rule.

When Moses descended from the mountain to present God's laws to the waiting Israelites, he discovered them carousing and worshiping an idol: a golden calf they'd sculpted from melted-down jewelry gathered from within their tribes. As if on cue, the Israelites demonstrated the evil that God described in the Second Commandment. In a fit of anger, Moses dashed the stone tablets the Lord had inscribed with the Ten Commandments. The aged leader pulverized the calf into powder, scattered it on the people's water source and ordered them to drink it. Then according to God's command, Moses told the Levites to slaughter friends, brothers, and neighbors who had participated in the calf ritual. Three thousand died that day. Later a plague inflicted the remaining Israelites, and Moses climbed the mountain again, blank stone tablets in hand, to ask God for another inscription of the commandments (Ex 31:18–32:30).

As a result, many Israelites striving to obey the Commandments did not create images of *Yahweh* or other religious figures. About fifteen-hundred years after the golden calf incident, the new Christians—Jews descended from the Israelite desert wanderers—understood the consequences of the Second Commandment, and the image question surfaced again. According to the church, what exactly was a graven image and what constituted worshiping it? As a follower of Jesus, released from the law, did they even need to ask? These questions riddled Christianity from its inception through the Reformation, rising and falling according to which clergy or ruler led the church in any given century.

The Pros and Cons

Christians against religious images pointed to the Second Commandment and the golden calf story. They believed images of deity and other religious figures encouraged idolatry. That is, worshiping the created thing rather than the spiritual being, the one true God in the form of the Trinity. They stood in favor of iconoclasm, a word originating from the Greek words *eikon* ("icon or image") and *klao* ("break or destroy"), which means the deliberate destruction of images. The iconoclasts ("haters of images") believed that wavering on the Second Commandment plunged them into idolatry and grievous sin.

In turn, iconodules ("lovers of images") who defended the use of images reminded their challengers that after the calf incident, God himself commissioned a sculpture, the snake on a cross, to heal his people (Num 21:4-9). Iconodules also quoted Pope Gregory the Great's response to iconoclasm in the early seventh century. He explained, "What writing presents to readers, a picture presents to the unlearned who view it, since in the image even the ignorant see what they ought to follow; in the picture the illiterate read." During the early Middle Ages, many churchgoers could not read, and only the privileged owned copies of Scripture. Consequently, images often served as didactic tools in churches and homes.

Despite protests from the clergy and the people, iconoclast rulers in early Byzantium banned representations of holy people and events for almost a century. Iconoclasts destroyed icons and other free-standing art, ripped apart illuminated manuscripts and whitewashed images or changed mosaics on church walls and ceilings. Sometimes they replaced these images with a cross, a sign that both sides of the dispute recognized as central to the faith. Some remaining crosses witness to this practice. For example, in the council chambers of Hagia Sophia in Istanbul, it's obvious that someone cut out images of saints and replaced them with medallions framing crosses.

The Church in Conflict

An illustration in the Khludov Psalter of the ninth century depicts iconoclasts whitewashing an icon of Jesus, perhaps preparing to replace it with a cross. It's a rare visual representation of Byzantine iconoclasm, secretly painted during the ban of sacred images. As an art history teacher, I appreciate the psalter's technical and historical value. But as a Christian, the illumination sorely reminds me of the many clashes between believers, reported in the New Testament and church history. The image debate wasn't just an ongoing discussion. It fostered hatred, destruction and in some cases, the

Iconoclasts in the *Khludov Psalter.*
State Historical Museum, Moscow.
Ninth century.

loss of lives. For the most part, the Byzantines didn't fight with Christians outside the Eastern tradition. They fought, ridiculed and ostracized one another.

However we feel about the clash between iconodules and iconoclasts, we can learn from their behavior. The hardest people to interact with peaceably can be the Christians in our own church, our own denomination or theological persuasion. Even with our similarities, their actions and opinions can dismay us. We need not just the image, but the peaceable power of Christ's cross to love one another, respect one another and disagree with one another.

PART 7

Enduring Mysteries

The Cross and Its Eternal Power

For the cross of Christ, which was set up for the salvation of mortals,
is both a mystery and an example: a sacrament whereby the Divine
power takes effect, an example whereby man's devotion is excited: for
to those who are rescued from the prisoner's yoke. Redemption fur-
ther procures the power of following the way of the cross by imitation.
How shall we share in the name of Christ save by being inseparably
united to Him, Who is, as He Himself asserted, "the Way, the Truth,
and the Life?"

POPE GREGORY THE GREAT

34

Pilgrims of the Cross

Blessed are those whose strength is in you, who have set their
hearts on pilgrimage. They go from strength to strength,
till each appears before God in Zion. —PSALM 84:5, 7

A Pilgrim Ampulla with a Cross

W HEN BISHOPS DEDICATED Jerusalem's Church of the Holy Sepulcher in the mid-fourth century, travel to the Holy Land increased. Early Christians wanted to visit the sites of their Savior's birth, death and resurrection, and pilgrimages quickened until the seventh century when Muslims seized the region. According to one historian, Christians wanted to "see, touch, and breathe the air of holy places and thereby fully experience their faith. Standing at these commemorative sites, they could identify with the figures they venerated and imagine that they themselves had participated in the fateful events of the past." When pilgrims touched the wood, stones and memorials, they believed these objects transmitted holiness to them.

In his letters, Saint Jerome, a doctor of the Latin church, described the spiritual pilgrimage of Paula, a wealthy Roman widow who devoted her life to study and good works. She traveled to Bethlehem and Jerusalem in the fourth century and examined the significant markers of Christ's life. Entering the grotto in Bethlehem, she envisioned Jesus in swaddling clothes, the magi adoring God, the magnificent star, the virgin mother, the "foster father" and the shepherds in the night. Visiting the Church of the Holy Sepulcher, Paula prostrated herself "in adoration before the cross and prayed as if she could see the Lord himself hanging from it. And when she entered the tomb, she kissed the stone which the angel had rolled away." She also kissed the place where the Lord had lain.

Much like Paula, early Christians embarked on inward, spiritual journeys during their pilgrimages to the Holy Land. Egeria, a nun from Spain or Southern Gaul, described the ritual she and companions instituted at sacred destinations. "For it was always customary with us that, whenever we succeeded in reaching the places we desired to visit, prayer should first be made there, then the lection should be read from the book, then one appropriate psalm should be said, then prayer should be made again," she wrote in her travel journal. "At God's bidding we always kept to this custom, whenever we were able to come to the places we desired."

These earliest recorded trips from the fourth century—before medieval pilgrimages became pathways to penance or indulgences—seem borne from a desire to draw close to Christ with worship and thanksgiving.

Trudging to Jerusalem

In their purest form pilgrimages to Jerusalem resisted the temptation to glorify places, objects or the pilgrims themselves. Based on miracle stories and the teachings of some church leaders, pilgrims considered their Holy Land travel a journey of the soul, linking the physical and spiritual worlds together. John Chrysostom, a fourth-century Greek church father, encouraged visits to even the "lifeless spots where the saints had lived." Avitus, the Bishop of Vienne, in the fifth century described "a place, far on the eastern side of the world where winter and summer didn't follow one another." But soon the expectations for a "heavenly touch" in the Holy Land grew so great, some church fathers began insisting that pilgrimages weren't necessary for holiness or answered prayer.

John Chrysostom backtracked at one point, saying there was no need "to cross the seas or fare upon a long journey; let each of us at home invoke God earnestly and He will hear our prayer." Around the same time, Gregory Nazianzen of Asia Minor wrote a short letter about these journeys. He referred to Christians who considered a visit to Jerusalem an essential ingredient of piety. The church father claimed that Christ never commanded this travel, although the tradition wasn't without merit. However, pilgrims placed themselves in harm's way and it was better to stay home.

Despite these cautions, the trips increased. For months pilgrims to Jerusalem trudged along dangerous roads in groups. Wildlife, bandits, bad weather, swindlers and hostile towns threatened journeys and lives. The sixth-century pilgrim of Piacenza, a Christian who recorded his sacred journeys, encountered unfriendly Judeans and Samaritans. He wrote,

> There were several Samaritan cities and villages on our way down through the plains, and wherever we passed along the streets they burned away our footprints with straw, whether we were Christians or Jews, they have such a horror of both. . . . When you arrive they curse you.

Determined pilgrims considered these dangers and humiliations merely the cost of traveling to the holy city and gazing on Christ's cross and tomb. Often when pilgrims reached Jerusalem, they kissed the ground.

Blessings from the Cross

After surviving the trip and touching sacred relics, pilgrims wanted mementos of their journeys. As a result, a craft industry sprung up to create religious souvenirs for travelers. In the sixth century wooden pilgrim boxes, with painted lids illustrating Christ's life, grew popular for storing small relics and keepsakes. Visitors also wanted to carry back a blessing to their homelands for healing or protection. To accomplish this, they carried small *ampullae* filled with oil so they could be blessed by what they believed was wood from Christ's cross. The Piacenza pilgrim recorded this process, observed at the Church of the Holy Sepulcher: "They offer oil to be blessed in little flasks. When the mouth of one of the little flasks touches the Wood of the Cross, the oil instantly bubbles over, and unless it is closed very quickly, it all spills out." Accordingly, archaeologists have discovered many *ampullae* with crosses carved on them.

Other common pilgrim mementos were small *eulogia* (blessing tokens) stamped with Christian images representing sacred places. For example, tokens with the three magi originated in Bethlehem, while those with two women standing near an empty tomb represented the Church of the Holy Sepulcher. Pilgrims believed these clay or earth tokens imparted blessing, healing and protection, including scraping the edges to scatter dust in endangered areas or mixing the particles with water and ingesting it.

In turn, pilgrims left behind personal belongings to honor Christ. The Piacenza pilgrim described mementos hanging near his tomb. "There are ornaments in vast numbers, which hang from the iron rods: armlets, bracelets, necklaces, rings, tiaras, plaited girdles, belts, emperors' crowns of gold and precious stones and the insignia of an empress." In a sense, even after departure pilgrims lingered at this sacred site.

Mapping a Personal Pilgrimage

As pilgrimages marched into the Middle Ages, they devolved from simple devotional journeys into extrabiblical rituals swathed in legalism, superstition, competition and commercialism. But ancient pilgrimages, despite their later problems, can still inspire us. We may never travel to Jerusalem or Rome or other historic locations, but we can create pilgrimages of our own, reliving and reviving our journey with God. The soul responds to physical places that recall significant spiritual junctures.

Mapping out a personal, spiritual pilgrimage begins with questions. Where did I first open my heart to God? Where did I vow to God or renew my commitment to him? Where did I intensely grow and change as a believer? Where did I marry or bury someone who influenced me spiritually? If I can't visit these locations, what collected photos and objects represent them? Can I handle these "souvenirs" again, creating a pilgrimage without travel?

If we approach meaningful locations and personal artifacts with reverence and reflection, with tears and laughter, we can resolve to carry on. We can renew our strength as pilgrims of the cross.

35

The Ecumenical Cross

But I, when I am lifted up from the earth,
will draw all men to myself. —JOHN 12:32

The Matthew Carpet Page
from the Lindisfarne Gospels

THE CELTS EMBRACED CHRISTIANITY with deep devotion and a wide streak of independence.

The Romans never conquered Ireland, so the Celts didn't assimilate the empire's culture to the extent of other lands. According to one historian, "Ireland had few walls and divided pastures, war was the sport of kings, Celtic women fought like Amazons, and marriage, as an institution, was largely ignored." Ireland maintained contacts with the Roman Empire through trade and travel, but when the Celts converted to Christianity, they preserved their culture's free spirit. Especially during the fourth through seventh centuries, they practiced a unique version of the faith, shaped by local customs and compromises.

Celtic monasteries, rather than Roman bishoprics, provided the structure for Christian communities. The ascetic monks feverishly pursued fasting, meditation, repentance and personal deprivation. They encouraged missionary outreaches throughout the world, and emphasized learning, writing, preserving great literature and creating beautiful illuminated manuscripts. But they also combined pagan rituals, beliefs and places with Christianity. Among the pagan practices, monks shaved their heads in the Druidic fashion, adopted cultic gods and goddesses and combined Christian and pagan holidays.

The Celts observed their peculiar Christianity for a few centuries primarily because the physical distance matched their philosophical separation from Rome. But eventually the two Christian groups repeatedly clashed, especially over the date of Easter and the style of tonsure (head shaving) for monks. Rome wanted unified practices throughout Christianity, and the Synod of Whitby in 664 settled the dispute. The Roman Christians won, but the Celts didn't easily comply. The situation required a diplomatic mediator to manage the change to Roman rites and begin healing the rift.

The Celtic-Roman Transition

Enter Cuthbert, the Prior of Melrose Abbey. He'd accepted the Whitby decision and church officials commissioned him to the Priory of Lindisfarne to ease the transition. "Cuthbert was a perfect choice for such a sensitive role; his reputation for devotion and sanctity, and the fact the he had been raised in the Celtic tradition and now supported Roman rule made his gentle leadership ideal for the job at hand," explains a British source. Cuthbert earned a reputation as a tactful, patient leader. He aligned Christian practices that really mattered and allowed other differences to remain. He also devoted much time to evangelism. Although some historians believe an early biographer practiced historical revisionism and overstated Cuthbert's influence, still today he's credited for a spirit of reconciliation.

After a dozen years Cuthbert retired from spiritual leadership to live as a contemplative hermit. Later he reluctantly returned to Lindisfarne to serve as its bishop, but died two years later. Cuthbert's tomb at the priory became a pilgrimage site, with visitors reporting miracles at his grave and dubbing him the "Wonder-Worker of England." Because of threats from Danish invaders, almost three-hundred years later monks transferred his bones to Durham Cathedral in England, where they remain today.

However, from an artistic standpoint the greatest memorial to Cuthbert belongs to the British Library in London.

A Masterpiece Manuscript

The Lindisfarne Gospels form one of the world's great illuminated manuscripts. This masterpiece was created in the early eighth century in Northumbria for ceremonial use and to celebrate Cuthbert's life. The manuscript's captivating artwork, intricate script and religious symbolism frame the four Gospels. With extraordinary skill and perseverance, Eadfrith, the Bishop of Lindisfarne from 698 to 721, copied and illustrated the text. Although books produced at Lindisfarne required teams of workers, Eadfrith labored alone as an artist-scribe, a privileged status.

"The making of the Lindisfarne Gospels is different, this is *opus dei,* the work for God elevated to a new level," comments Michelle Brown, curator of illuminated manuscripts at the British Library. She compares making the Lindisfarne Gospels to Cuthbert "engaging in his personal inner struggle with his demons—not just for his own soul's redemption, but as a corporate endeavor on behalf of all humanity." Monastics believed the scribe preached with his fingers, fulfilling a sacred role and actively ministering to a community and beyond.

Befitting a "work for God," the Lindisfarne Gospels prominently celebrate the cross on its carpet pages, introducing each of the gospel books: Matthew, Mark, Luke and John. According to tradition, carpet pages prepare readers to enter the "sacred ground" of a gospel and issue a call to prayer. Carpet pages earned this name because their intricate design resembled oriental rugs. Most likely, illustrators intended this resemblance because religious devotees used prayer mats in Northumbria, Eastern Christianity and Islam, and their influence had reached Lindisfarne.

"Embedded within [the carpet page] is the sign of the cross, with many other crosses hidden again in different parts of these carpet pages," observes Brown. "The fact that it is not a physical body suspended on a crucifix does not mean that it is less sophisticated." Instead, Eadfrith's masterful design displays a high level of artistic and symbolic accomplishment.

In a stunning ecumenical gesture, each of the carpet pages features a different type of cross, representing varying church traditions. The artist-scribe also integrated decorative styles from diverse cultures. The British Library website explains:

> You could tell a Pict, a Copt, a Frank, an Angle, or a Saxon by their appearance. Dress and jewellery [sic] could signal identity, belief and status in well-recognised ways. We do the same today. Visual references in the Lindisfarne Gospels would have been widely understood. Bringing them together in one book brought a sense of cohesion and identity to a new Christian nation.

In effect, the Lindisfarne Gospels respected varied Christian cultures and positioned their differences around the cross.

Cuthbert's spirit of reconciliation seems to emanate from the varied Lindisfarne crosses. They can inspire us toward peace and cooperation with Christians who celebrate traditions different than ours. Instead of focusing on our differences, we can share our common beliefs and respect for the cross.

36

Desperately Seeking Sanctuary

For the message of the cross is foolishness to those who are perishing, but
to us who are being saved it is the power of God. —1 CORINTHIANS 1:18

A Sanctuary Boundary Marker

THE TOWERING DURHAM CATHEDRAL ranks as Europe's most important Romanesque church. It's a World Heritage Site and considered
"the greatest Norman building in England, perhaps even in Europe." Its
size and architectural detail stagger the mind. Its cultural and spiritual
histories loom large and legendary. But during the Middle Ages the
beauty and grandeur probably didn't faze an Anglo-Saxon in deep trou-
ble. He just wanted to reach the church in time to save his life.

By English law, Durham Cathedral participated in the sanctuary
tradition. When a criminal or debtor wanted to escape arrest, he
could plead for asylum at the cathedral, if he arrived before pursuing
authorities caught him. The runaway banged on the cathedral's north
door, using the enormous bronze sanctuary knocker shaped like the
head of an ugly griffin and better suited for a Viking ship than a sacred

entrance. Then the fugitive desperately clung to the knocker's ring, waiting for someone to usher him in and toll the church bell to notify Durham's citizens that a felon sought sanctuary. (At night, two men waited in a room above the north door, looking for sanctuary seekers arriving in the dark.) If anyone in the realm violated a person's right to sanctuary, the church-at-large excommunicated him.

Once inside, the criminal confessed his crime to a priest, surrendered his weapons, paid a nominal fee and donned a black gown. He lived in a railed-off alcove above the southwest tower, and within thirty-seven days decided whether to stand trial or leave the country. If a criminal chose to "quit the kingdom," the law afforded him nine days to exit England's borders, traveling solely on the king's highways. For the journey, he wore nothing on his head and a long white robe. He carried only a wooden cross.

The Medieval Right to Sanctuary

England's medieval sanctuary law, practiced by designated churches throughout the kingdom, actually formed its roots in pagan and Jewish practices. In Egyptian, Greek and Roman temples, the *cella* (room with a statue of the honored god) could protect criminals or refugees seeking sanctuary. The Old Testament mentions six cities of refuge for those who unintentionally murdered someone (Num 35:6). Later, toward the end of the fourth century AD, the Roman government recognized Christian sanctuary laws for churches, adopting the ancient belief that sacred spaces were impenetrable and contagious. Someone "in sanctuary" had entered a holy place that could not be violated, and under its influence, he might spiritually transform.

This protection, though banned for a short period because of abuse, carried into the Middle Ages and countries beyond England. The earliest written documentation of English sanctuary appeared in the dooms (laws) of the Anglo-Saxon king Æthelbert in 600. Later, the types of crimes allowed, the extent of protection, the ritual for obtaining sanctuary and the punishment for violation varied according to locations and rulers. One law distinguished between accidental and premeditated murder. In some churches, the fugitive needed to sit on a *frith* (peace stool) near the altar to gain sanctuary.

Norman kings legislated two kinds of sanctuary churches: a general sanctuary for all churches and a chartered sanctuary for selected churches. A charter granted immunity for life, even for those who committed high treason. Over time, a court poet, a pretender to the throne and even royal family members rushed to sanctuary to avoid a king's hostility. Not even a sovereign could yank his relatives out of a church. In some places, violating sanctuary led to capital punishment.

Whatever the details, the sanctuary principle remained the same: if you've committed a horrible crime, run to the church for protection. During this anxious journey, signs of the cross often pointed the way. Stone crosses inscribed with the word *Sancturarium* stood as signposts along the highways, leading sinners to their haven. In some locations, crosses also marked the boundaries of church land, and stepping within this area assured safety. Sometimes crosses themselves provided sanctuary. In eleventh-century Scotland, when certain clansmen who committed unintended murder touched the MacDuff Cross, they escaped punishment from outsiders (those not under the earl of Fife's jurisdiction). For the sinner aware of his crime, the sign of the cross meant mercy.

Unfortunately, sanctuary laws could be abused. Experienced criminals committed offenses intentionally, risking night flights to cathedrals. To peaceful citizens and government authorities, it seemed unfair for lawbreakers to hide in churches. When priests released criminals to exit a country, some "penitents" dodged the king's highway and escaped into the unknown. Through the centuries violations increased, with armed invaders storming cathedrals and capturing law breakers. In the twelfth century, a sanctuary law didn't deter the king's henchmen from murdering Archbishop Thomas Becket at Canterbury Cathedral. By the Reformation, sanctuary rights fell out of favor, and the last laws disappeared in England and Europe by the seventeenth and eighteenth centuries.

The Broad Door of Grace

Medieval sanctuary laws forgave horrific crimes and blessed the repentant offenders with a clean start. It's difficult for our postmodern mindset to condone this protection. We can understand political sanctuary from ruthless dictators, but offering asylum to criminals? Their presence taints a community, a country. Moral law breakers should be punished. We do not like such lavish compassion.

Thankfully, God does not think like us. His love for humanity flows deeper and wider than we can imagine. So does his mercy. Early medieval sanctuary laws can only faintly reflect the Sovereign's endless patience. Whatever sin we commit, however many times we fail, he forgives us. God waits in the night of our souls, swinging open his broad door of grace when we flee to him and repent. He accepts us however we arrive: sweaty from the escape, wild-eyed with fear, the blood-stench of crime on our sleeves and doubting that sanctuary from sin—our haunting spiritual crimes—actually exists.

Still, we can believe it. During the medieval sanctuary process, signs of the cross accompanied sinners in and out of asylum, stepping them toward an altered life. In turn, Christ's cross bears the promise of forgiveness, helping us find refuge in God's grace. Even more, God doesn't banish us from his kingdom or force us to stand trial. When we slip back into life, spiritually we are totally free, utterly impeachable. Wearing robes of white, carrying the sign of the cross—the mark of the King's forgiveness—we can begin again.

37

Hearts Up

Consider him who endured such opposition from sinful men, so that you will not grow weary and lose heart. —HEBREWS 12:3

The Fleschi Morgan Reliquary

It's a small box with a big message.

About the size of a shirt pocket, the Fleschi Morgan Reliquary—a masterful creation of cloisonné enamel—distinguishes itself among Byzantine metalworks. Crafted in the ninth century in Constantinople, it celebrates not just Christ's crucifixion but also the abundant and eternal life he promised to his followers.

"[This piece] consolidates in a little portable box the grand message of salvation," observes the art historian Thomas F. Mathews. "On the cover the crucified Christ stands erect and triumphant, his eyes wide open. Sun and moon bear witness to his miraculous death, flowers spring up on all sides, and his powerful outstretched arms shelter the nascent church below."

Standing under Christ, Mary the virgin and John the apostle represent the early church, and the busts of twenty-seven saints decorate the silver-gilt lid and sides. The lid's underside divides into four scenes from Christ's life: the Annunciation, Nativity, Crucifixion and *Anastasis* (Resurrection). Turned over, the back features a framed, outlined cross. According to Mathews, the box's cumulative message is life-giving. He interprets the message as, "Christ descended into hell to bring humanity back to life."

Prior to Christ's arrest and crucifixion, he told the disciples, "The Son of Man must suffer many things and be rejected by the elders, chief priests and teachers of the law, and he must be killed and on the third day be raised to life" (Lk 9:22). Christ foretold his resurrection, but as he languished on the cross, or while his body stiffened in the sepulcher, the disciples faced a crisis of confidence. It's difficult to imagine abundant life when looking at a loved one's sealed tomb. The early church faced the same dilemma during the emperors' persecutions. It's hard to smell heaven's sweetness when surrounded by death's defiant stench.

Of course, the disciples soon touched, talked and walked with the risen Christ. With heads up, they watched his ascension. But how did early Christians hold to the Lord's promise of life? They lifted up their hearts.

Hearts Up to the Lord

One of the oldest liturgical versions of the Lord's Supper instructed Christians to bring their hearts to the weekly bread-and-wine remembrance of Christ's death. The *Church Order of Hippolytus,* written in the third century, initiated the sacrament with this exchange and prayer:

Bishop:	The Lord be with you.
Congregation:	And with thy spirit.
Bishop:	Hearts up.
Congregation:	We have them to the Lord
Bishop:	Let us give thanks to the Lord.
Congregation:	It is meet and right.

Bishop: We thank thee, God, through Thy beloved
                     Servant Jesus Christ, whom in the last times
                     Thou hast sent us as Savior and Redeemer and
                     Messenger of Thy counsel, the Logos who
                     comes from Thee, through whom Thou hast
                     made all things, the virgin, and in her body
                     He became flesh and was shown forth as Thy
                     Son, born of the Holy Spirit and the virgin.
                     To fulfill Thy will and to prepare Thee a holy
                     people, he stretched out his hands, when he
                     suffered, that he might release from suffering
                     those who have believed on Thee.

Whatever life on earth had served that week, on the Sabbath these early Christians lifted their hearts to the Lord. The liturgy didn't ask them to "listen up" or focus the mind, but to bring the heart—the repository of private thoughts, deepest longings and hidden fears—to the Lord. Full of joy or grief, doubt or gratitude, worry or wonder, they remembered Christ's sacrifice. He suffered to release them from suffering. He died so they could live. Like the message of the reliquary, the hope of eternal life infused their spirits so they would "not grow weary and lose heart" (Heb 12:3).

Evidently, this bishop's prayer provided the framework for Eucharist prayers written in successive centuries. Echoing the ancient congregation, "It is meet and right." Every generation of Christians needs encouragement. We want the assurance that Christ's sacrifice will someday release us from this world's worries. To remember his presence and promise, like the early believers we can—weekly, daily, hourly—lift up our hearts.

38

The Veiled Cross

"They divided my garments among them and cast lots for my clothing."So this is what the soldiers did. —JOHN 19:24

A Veiled Cross for Good Friday

Eₐʀʟʏ ᴏɴ, ᴛʜᴇ Eɴɢʟɪsʜ ᴅɪsᴘʟᴀʏᴇᴅ a flair for the dramatic. Long before Shakespeare, a tenth-century Good Friday liturgy drew worshipers into the tragedy of God forsaking his Son on the cross. Taken from the *Regularis Concordia,* a Benedictine monastic code created for "the English nation," the service integrated biblical enactment and songs into the liturgical readings. Many scholars believe the roots of Western theater reach back to this solemn ceremony and its "stripping of the altar."

In the afternoon on Good Friday, the service began with prayerful silence, followed by readings from the Old Testament books of Exodus and Hosea. The prophet Hosea set a repentant, prophetic tone for the liturgy.

Come, let us return to the LORD.

He has torn us to pieces

    but he will heal us;

he has injured us

    but he will bind up our wounds.

After two days he will revive us;

    on the third day he will restore us,

    that we may live in his presence. (Hos 6:1-2)

To this plea the Lord replied, "Your love is like the morning mist, / like the early dew that disappears. . . . / For I desire mercy, not sacrifice, / and acknowledgement of God / rather than burnt offerings" (Hos 6:4, 6).

After responses from the psalms and prayers, a friar read the Passion account from the Gospel of John. According to instructions in the *Regularis Concordia,* during this reading two deacons stalked the altar "like thieves." When the reader reached the sentence "They divided my garments among them" (Jn 19:24), the deacons stripped away the altar cloth lying under the Gospel book, spoiling the sacred arrangement. Both the altar and the book represented Christ's presence. So in essence, the deacons assaulted the Lord's body before his death, mimicking ruthless Roman guards. Intercessory prayers followed the Passion reading and prepared congregants for honoring the cross.

Next, during mournful songs, monks placed a cloth-covered cross in front of the altar. The lyrics asked, "My people, what have I done to you?" with the response, "Holy God, Holy and Strong, Holy Immortal One, have mercy on us!" Gradually, monks unveiled the cross and placed it on a cushion. The *Regularis Concordia* directed, "As soon as it has been unveiled, the abbot shall come before the holy Cross and shall prostrate himself thrice with all the brethren of the right hand side of the choir, that is, seniors and juniors; and with deep and heartfelt sighs shall say the seven penitential psalms and the prayers in the honor of the Holy Cross."

Retelling the Resurrection

Denuding the altar, mourning through song and repenting with sighs recalled the agony of Christ's death, but the ritual also prepared Christians for Easter Sunday's triumph. After congregants mourned Christ, deacons wrapped the cross in a cloth and buried it in an improvised sepulcher, a curtain drawn around part of the altar. The written instructions required that "the holy Cross shall be guarded with all reverence until the night of the Lord's Resurrection. And during the night let brethren be chosen by twos and threes, if the community be large enough, who shall keep faithful watch, chanting psalms."

Before the congregation returned for Easter Sunday mass, a monk removed the cross, leaving behind the linen cloth. On Easter Sunday the drama reached its joyous conclusion. Three monks dressed in copes (capelike vestments) represented the three Marys carrying spices, and another monk wearing an alb played the angel at Christ's tomb. They recited the biblical questions and answers at the empty sepulchre.

"Whom do you seek?" asked the angel.

"Jesus of Nazareth," the women replied.

"He is not here. He is risen," said the angel.

The resurrection angel sang to the three Marys, "Come and see the place [where the Lord had been laid, alleluia]." He lifted the curtain and revealed an empty tomb, except for Christ's shroud left behind. The *Regularis Concordia* instructed the monks to "take up the shroud and spread it out before the clergy; and, as if demonstrating that the Lord has risen and is not now wrapped in it, let them sing this antiphon: The Lord has risen from the sepulcher. . . . And let them lay the cloth upon the altar."

Then the church bells rang. In word and deed, Christ had risen.

Glorying in the Cross Today

Many features of the dramatic Good Friday service from the *Regularis*

Concordia survive in today's liturgies. Ceremonies begin with solemn silence and end with splendid anticipation. Whatever our worship tradition, the Good Friday liturgy and its anthems can draw us to the ultimate joy of the cross. Can we proclaim,

> We glory in your cross, O Lord,
> and praise and glorify your holy resurrection;
> for by virtue of your cross
> joy has come to the whole world.
>   May God be merciful to us and bless us,
> show us the light of his countenance, and come to us.
>   Let you ways be known upon earth,
> your saving health among all nations.
>   Let the peoples praise you, O God;
> let all the people praise you.
>   We glory in your cross, O Lord,
> and praise and glorify your holy resurrection;
> for by virtue of your cross
> joy has come to the world.

39

The Eternal Kingdom

His kingdom will never end. —LUKE 1:33

**The Crown of the
Holy Roman Empire**

CHRISTMAS DAY 800 MARKED one of the turning points in European history. Charles, King of the Franks, attended the third Nativity mass at St. Peter's Basilica in Rome. He prostrated himself for prayer at the Tomb of the Apostle, in front of the congregation. When Charles rose from his petitions, Pope Leo III stepped forward and crowned him emperor of the Romans. The assemblage cried out, "Long life and victory to Charles, the most pious Augustus, the great, peace-loving emperor, crowned by God." Then everyone in attendance, including the pope, bowed to the new emperor, also known as Charlemagne.

Historians debate whether Charlemagne expected the simple coronation or it caught him by surprise. In any event, the holiday ceremony created a church-state alliance. Politically, spiritually and artistically, Charlemagne pursued the power and style of the Roman Empire that had crumbled with the abdication of Romulus Augustulus in the fifth century. The new Carolingian emperor ruled the Western world, and literature celebrated his seemingly unlimited sovereignty.

The twelfth century writer of the *Couronnement de Louis,* claimed, "When God elected ninety-nine kingdoms, He put the best of all in sweet France. The best king was called Charlemagne; With all his heart he aggrandized sweet France. God made no land that didn't depend on him." Through the centuries stories about Charlemagne's reign turned mythic, and it's sometimes hard to separate fact from fiction. Still, Charlemagne influenced the rise of the Holy Roman Empire that eventually transferred to German rule and lasted almost a thousand years.

Imperial Regalia and the Cross

With the pomp and circumstance of ages past, each advent of a new emperor for this empire required royal regalia for the coronation. At the ceremony the emperor received the Crown of the Holy Empire. Eventually an orb, lance and imperial cross became treasured parts of the regalia, added over several centuries. To emphasize the "holy" nature of the empire, these pieces featured representations of Christ's cross.

The most important object in the regalia, the bejeweled crown was probably created during the tenth century, with the cross added later in the eleventh century. Octagon in shape, the crown supports eight gold plates: four decorated with pearls and precious jewels and four with kingly figures from the Old and New Testaments, fired and filled with cloisonné enamel. The figures include David, Solomon, Hezekiah and Jesus. Currently the Hofburg Imperial Palace in Vienna, Austria, displays the original crown, with replicas in other European museums.

Although the number of objects in the regalia grew along with the empire, the earliest, core pieces referred to Christ's cross. Metalworkers embedded the lance with nail shards, reportedly from the Savior's cross. A cross topped the *globus crucifer* (golden orb), depicting Christ's dominion over the world. The lustrous imperial cross served as a reliquary for wood presumed to be from Christ's cross. These decorative regalia crosses represented an emperor's right to rule under God, but unfortunately, not many rulers remembered this. They used their power to conquer and destroy others while glorifying themselves.

In the eighteenth century the writer and atheist Voltaire looked back and cynically quipped that the Holy Roman Empire was neither holy, Roman or an empire. Greed, slaughter, intolerance, adultery, jealousies, competition, warmongering and other sins permeated the "holy" millennia. The empire's power didn't stretch to Rome, and it really constituted a union of territories. Like all earthly kingdoms, the Holy Roman Empire fell short of its claims, its conquering ideal.

Ironically, the cross-decorated regalia lasted longer than the proclaimed empire and its emperors. But someday these glittering prizes could disappear too. When we observe them through museum glass or on the pages of art books, we're reminded that nothing crafted from human hands lasts forever. Only the kingdom of God endures.

The Kingdom of God

Jesus often taught about the kingdom of God, that its values contradict the power-grabbing of the world's empires. In Matthew 5:3-10, Scripture records one of his most poetic and poignant teachings about this kingdom and its citizens.

> Blessed are the poor in spirit,
>   for theirs is the kingdom of heaven.
> Blessed are those who mourn,
>   for they will be comforted.
> Blessed are the meek,
>   for they will inherit the earth.

Blessed are those who hunger and thirst for righteousness,
for they will be filled.
Blessed are the merciful,
for they will be shown mercy.
Blessed are the pure in heart,
for they will see God.
Blessed are the peacemakers,
for they will be called sons of God.
Blessed are those who are persecuted because of righteousness,
for theirs is the kingdom of heaven.

According to Jesus, members of God's kingdom are poor, mournful, meek, hungry, thirsty, merciful, pure, peaceful and persecuted. I've been a Christian since childhood, and I still don't comprehend the blessedness of these beatitudes. Everywhere, the culture tells me to live against the grain of these teachings. When I'm poor, I'm to get rich quick. When I'm mournful, I'm to "buck up." When I'm meek, I'm to assert myself. If I hunger and thirst for righteousness, I'm too conservative. When I'm merciful, I didn't receive what's "due" to me. When I'm pure, I'm straight-laced. When I'm peaceful, I don't care enough. When I'm persecuted, I should fight back. I've been handed this advice from "the world," but most of it generated from Christians. I've offered this advice myself.

Jesus invited us to live in an inverted kingdom. In this kingdom the first shall be last, childlike faith is necessary for citizenship and it's hard for a rich person to enter the gates. He also claimed that the kingdom of God is near, as near as the cross he would soon carry. As near as our willingness to repent and allow his kingdom to live within us.

40

To Rise Again

On the third day he will rise again. —LUKE 18:33

A Cross from the Hill of Crosses

If a strong wind sweeps the Lithuanian landscape, tourists can hear the Hill of Crosses before actually spotting it. A multitude of crosses planted in the ground will sway, clank and rattle, beckoning them toward a grassy mound on the left bank of the River Kulpé in Šiauliai County. Walking toward the hill, an old cliché reverses itself. It can be difficult "seeing the trees for the forest." The haphazard arrangements cluster so densely, they look like dark masses rather than individual signs of the cross. Drawing closer, the number of fascinating crosses, crucifixes, Christ images, effigies and mementos evokes a quiet, almost eerie reverence.

Centuries ago, Lithuanians began staking crosses on this hillside as statements of faith, nationality and remembrance. Over the centuries the crosses grew so crammed together they piled on one another and spilled into the meadow below. Large and small, majestic and humble,

The Hill of Crosses. Siauliai County, Lithuania. Unknown origin.

wood and metal, these crosses fashion a sacred space like nowhere else in the world.

Conflicting legends suggest why Lithuanians began staking crosses in the ground at this unassuming location. The hill might have been the backdrop for pagan worship, so medieval Christians reclaimed it by planting the first cross. Others say Lithuanians built a defensive fort on the hill and Teutonic Knights later destroyed it. Even though no written evidence exists, it's probable that countrymen erected crosses to memorialize insurgents who fought against Tsarist rule in 1831 and in 1863-1864. Old photographs from the nineteenth century show about 130 crosses on the hill's summit.

In the 1950s Communism ruled the country and it's certain that Lithuanians returning from Siberian gulags planted crosses to remember friends and family who died in exile. Clamping down on these signs of faith and protest, Communists burned or melted the crosses, bulldozed the ground, blocked roads to the hill and patrolled the site. Despite these extreme measures, crosses cropped up again, in increasing numbers. At least three more times authorities razed the hillside, but crosses kept reappearing.

After the fall of the Soviet Union, pilgrims from around the world began visiting the hill that today supports thousands and thousands of crosses. Many new crosses join the haphazard-looking monument each day, especially during the Easter season. Nobody legislates the cross-planting process; it springs from the hearts of people who honor their Christian faith, remember the dead and cherish freedom. Metaphorically, the irrepressible Hill of Crosses gained a life of its own, bearing a symbol of humanity's desire to rise again.

The Desire to Rise Again

Like crosses planted in the hard-won Lithuanian soil, we carry within us the desire to rise again. When life reverses itself, when health wavers, when we suffer through loss, the spirit wants to overcome, to recapture life, to regain the true self. We hope that floundering projects will turn around, that financial deficits will grow into prosperity, that bodies will heal and strengthen, that nations will rally and rebuild. We harbor the hope to crawl up or be pulled out of our deepest pits.

This rising-again desire patterns after Christ. Before his death, "he began to teach [his disciples] that the Son of Man must suffer many things and be rejected by the elders, chief priests and teachers of the law, and that he must be killed and after three days rise again" (Mt 8:31). After the suffering, Jesus rose from the grave into a new life. For forty days he walked and talked with his followers, restoring their faith in his life-saving message. Like Christ, we want to rise up from suffering. We need renewal. With his sustenance, we long to journey again, to live fully.

Since the dawn of Christianity, the cross has represented this longing, this determination, to regain life. For example, the early church initiated the practice of anointing the sick, applying oil in the shape of the cross. During the Middle Ages, while defending families, properties and kingdoms, warriors from Christian lands often wore armor decorated with the cross. In 1881, when Clara Barton founded an American society to protect the war-wounded, and later those ravished by natural disasters, she named it The Red Cross. After Lithuania gained independence in 1991, citizens who died standing for freedom or helped to restore the repressed nation received the distinguished Order of the Cross of Vytis. The sign of the cross honors the soul's ability to rise up during adversity, to transform again and again.

However, if we can no longer recover on earth, we crave the assurance of a rewarding afterlife, releasing our sorrows and reuniting with loved ones in heaven's light.

New Life in the Afterlife

A burial cave near the Mount of Olives in Jerusalem dates to the first century and contains many ossuaries (stone caskets) holding bones of the deceased. First discovered in the 1950s, researchers thought markings on the ossuaries were crosses. Coupled with common New Testament names etched in the stone, it seemed they'd discovered one of the oldest Jewish-Christian burial sites. Since this discovery, scholars have contested the suppositions about these crosses, claiming the small cross markings probably indicated how to position lids on the ossuaries. Despite the debate, some Christian groups still believe that long ago, the first believers scratched crosses in the forgotten *Dominus Flevit* cemetery.

Based on the proliferation of gravesite crosses found through two millennia, somewhere in early Christianity someone etched, carved, molded or planted the first cross on a tombstone or near a grave. This symbol not only memorialized the deceased, but staked the belief that the dead in Christ will rise again. The apostle Paul had written, "Listen, I tell you a mystery: We will not all sleep, but we will all be changed. . . . For the trumpet will sound, the dead will be raised imperishable, and we will be changed. For the perishable must clothe itself with the imperishable, and the mortal with immortality" (1 Cor

15:51-53). Christians expected to follow the path of their Lord who, forty days after the Resurrection, rose to heaven (Mk 16:19). After a journey through death, they would rise up to eternal life with him.

We cling to this same hope. The cross symbolizes the desire to rise again on earth. The cross promises we'll rise again to live in heaven. This is the mystery of the cross.

Notes

Introduction
Page 15   The apostle Paul wrote: Ephesians 3:4-6.

Page 15   "By means of a tree": David W. Bercot, ed., *A Dictionary of Early Christian Beliefs* (Peabody, Mass.: Hendrickson, 1998), p. 184.

Chapter 1: The Mystery of the Megalith
Page 19   In the nineteenth century: M. Scott Peck, *In Search of Stones* (New York: Hyperion, 1995), pp. 294, 298.

Page 19   With almost a thousand: "Introduction to Megalithic Sites in the U.K. and Eire," Megalithia website (2006) <www.megalithia.com/intro.html>.

Page 20   The inner circle features a sunken grave: Evan Hadingham, *Circles and Standing Stones* (New York: Walker and Company, 1975), p. 100.

Page 20   Given the grouping's size and shape: Aubrey Burl, *Rings of Stone* (New Haven, Conn.: Ticknor & Fields, 1979), p. 134.

Page 20   Several legends have developed: Except for the playing legend, these stories appear in Burl, *Rings of Stone,* p. 134. The playing story is from Peck, *In Search of Stones,* p. 294.

Page 21   During the nineteenth century, the site: Hadingham, *Circles and Standing Stones,* p. 98.

Page 21   "In severall [sic] places": Leonard A. Morrison, *History of John Morrison* (Boston: A. Williams and Company, 1880), pp. 19-20.

Page 21   Based on the Bronze Age timeframe: Jean-Pierre Mohen, *The World of Megaliths* (New York: Facts on File, 1989), pp. 101-4.

Page 21   One writer observed: Hadingham, *Circles and Standing Stones,* p. 100.

Chapter 2: Egyptian Signs of Life
Page 24   "May you awake in peace!": Rose-Marie and Rainer Hagen, *Egypt: Peo-*

                ple, Gods, Pharaohs (Köln: Taschen, 2003), pp. 200, 202. The story about Amun, the priest, the pharaoh and the *ankh* is from this source.

Page 24   "Truly, I am a servant of god": Ibid., p. 202.

Page 25   "full of tombs and corpses": Ibid.

Page 25   "I give you life": Ibid.

Page 25   They've suggested everything: Richard H. Wilkinson, *Reading Egyptian Art: A Hieroglyphic Guide to Ancient Egyptian Paintings and Sculpture* (London: Thames and Hudson, 1992), p. 177.

Page 25   For example, an entrance to King Sahure's funerary temple: John P. O'Neill, *Egyptian Art in the Age of the Pyramids* (New York: The Metropolitan Museum of Art, 1999), pp. 338-39.

Page 26   "We give you all life, stability and dominion": Ibid., p. 338.

Page 26   Not far away, a relief sculpture: Wilkinson, *Reading Egyptian Art*, p. 176.

Page 26   The gods also poured *ankhs* over monarchs: Ibid., p. 177.

Page 26   "that which sees the face": Katharine Stoddert Gilbert, Joan K. Holt and Sara Hudson, *Treasures of Tutankhamun* (New York: The Metropolitan Museum of Art, 1976), p. 140.

Page 26   During the Middle Kingdom: Ibid., p. 141.

Page 27   In the fourth-century Coptic Liturgy: "The Coptic Liturgy of Saint Basil," Coptic Network website (2008) <www.coptic.net/prayers/StBasilLiturgy.html>.

Page 27   "for salvation, remission of sins": Ibid.

Chapter 3: The Healing Cross

Page 29   the snake—associated with sin, evil, death, and deception: A serpent played a deceptive role in the story about humanity's fall from grace into sin and death (Gen 3:1-16). Both ancient Jews and early Christians were familiar with this story.

Page 29   According to mythology's timeline: This time frame is a general estimate. Biblical scholars place the exodus led by Moses at about 1446 BC and mythology claims Asclepius was born around 1363 or 1285 BC. See the *Life Application Bible, New International Version* (Wheaton, Ill., and Grand Rapids, Mich.: Tyndale House and Zondervan, 1991), p. 103. Also the website Mythical Chronology of Greece (2008) <www.mlahanas.de/Greeks/Mythology/MythicalChronology.html>. The mythology website explains, "This Mythical Chronology of Greece depicts the traditional chronology established for the events of ancient Greek mythology by ancient chronographers and mythographers. This list largely reflects the work of Saint Jerome, whose work in turn was based primarily on the analysis of Apollodorus, Diodorus Siculus, and Eusebius. In a few cases, the chronology also reflects the opinions of more recent scholars, who have cross-referenced the mythology to archeological discoveries." This chronology doesn't assume that the mythical characters actually existed.

Page 29   A myth claims the centaur Chiron: Stories about Asclepius vary. This version draws from Michael Lahanas, Greek and Roman Mythology (2008) <www.mlahanas.de/Greeks/Mythology/Chiron. html>.

Page 30   "Why did . . . Moses . . . exhibit a bronze": David W. Bercot, ed., *A Dictionary of Early Christian Beliefs* (Peabody, Mass.: Hendrickson, 1998), p. 610.

Pages 30-31   "Seest thou the cause of the Crucifixion": John Chrysostom, "Homily XXVII, Homilies on the Gospel of St. John and Epistle to the Hebrews," Christian Classics Ethereal Library website (2005) <www.ccel.org/ccel/schaff/npnf114.iv.xxix.html>.

Chapter 4: Ugly Roman Power Symbols

Page 32   The Roman stoic philosopher Seneca: Lucius Annaeus Seneca, *Moral Epistles Volume III,* trans. Richard M. Gummere (Cambridge, Mass.: Harvard University Press, 1925), pp. 161-67.

Page 33   "a most miserable death": Flavius Josephus, *The New Complete Works of Josephus,* trans. William Whiston, comp. Paul Maier (Grand Rapids: Kregel, 1999), p. 923.

Page 33   "the soldiers out of the wrath": Ibid., p. 874.

Page 33   Also in the first century, the Emperor Caligula: Joe Zias, "Crucifixion in Antiquity" <www.joezias.com/rucifixion/Antiquity.html>; Dr. James Tabor, The Jewish Roman World of Jesus web-site (1998) <www.religiousstudies.uncc.edu/jdtabor/crucifixion.html>.

Page 33   Before the Emperor Constantine banned crucifixion: Harold F. Vos, "The History of Crucifixion," *Nelson's New Illustrated Bible Manners and Customs* (Nashville: Thomas Nelson, 1999), p. 439.

Page 33   "practiced impalement": Ibid.

Page 33   The Greeks, Phoenicians and Carthaginians: Ibid.

Page 34   Most ancient secular writers omitted: Ibid., pp. 441-43. These pages describe the crucifixion process presented in this chapter.

Page 34   Christ could have been nailed: J. B. Torrance, "Cross, Crucifixion," in *New Bible Dictionary,* ed. I. Howard Marshall, A. R. Millard, J. I. Packer and D. J. Wiseman (Downers Grove, Ill.: InterVarsity Press, 1982), p. 246.

Page 35   "So they left the crucified to die": *Nelson's New Illustrated Bible Man-*

ners and Customs, p. 443.

Page 35   Or it was thrown on a garbage heap: Zias, "Crucifixion in An-
               tiquity."

Page 35   "The young hero stripped himself": Michael Swanton, ed., *The
               Dream of the Rood* (New York: Barnes, 1970), n.p.

Page 36   "Making remembrance of his life-giving sufferings": Robert Louis
               Wilken, *The Spirit of Early Christian Thought* (New Haven, Conn.:
               Yale University Press, 2003), p. 25.

Chapter 5: Shouldering the Cross

Page 39   Later officers struck: See John 18:22-23; Mark 14:65; Matthew
               27:26, 29-31.

Pages 39-40   Rufus and Alexander: See Mark 15:20-21.

Page 40   "a gardener, just returning home": Anne Catherine Emmerich, *The
               Dolorous Passion of Our Lord Jesus Christ* (London: Burns and Lambert,
               1862), p. 241.

Page 40   "Simon was much annoyed": Ibid.

Page 42   "We are persuaded": David W. Bercot, ed., *A Dictionary of Early
               Christian Beliefs* (Peabody, Mass.: Hendrickson, 1998), p. 243.

Chapter 6: The Garden and Golgotha

Page 44   "Moses flung his staff upon the ground": "Aaron's Rod," *The Jewish
               Encyclopedia* (New York: Funk & Wagnalls, 1901-1906), p. 6.

Page 45   In turn, rabbinical literature and the haggadah: Ibid, p. 5.

Page 45   "The staff with which Jacob crossed the Jordon": Ibid.

Page 45   Beginning its story earlier than the midrash: Ibid.

Page 45   *The Book of the Bee:* Earnest A. Wallis Budge, ed. and trans. (Oxford:
               Clarendon, 1886), pp. 50-59.

Page 47   "the rod of Moses, with which he subdued": *Jewish Encyclopedia,* p. 6.

Chapter 7: Inscription Insights

Page 49   Despite a flurry of accusations: Two gospel accounts differ on
               whether Jesus spoke again. As depicted in this introduction, Mat-
               thew 27:11-14 records the incident as if Jesus stayed silent through-
               out the accusations and didn't speak. John 18:33-37 records a longer
               conversation between Pilate and Jesus, about kingship. In John
               19:10-11, the ruler and the prisoner exchange words again, about
               the power God granted to Pilate.

Page 50   These languages included: *Life Application Bible, New International
               Version* (Wheaton, Ill., and Grand Rapids, Mich.: Tyndale House
               and Zondervan, 1991), p. 1924.

Page 50   When Samuel the great judge retired: For the full story about Sam-
               uel and Saul, read 1 Samuel 8:1–10:1.
Page 51   David "destroyed the enemies": This is quoted from Sirach 47:7, 11.
               King James Version of the Holy Bible, Christian Classics Ethereal
               Library website (2005) <www.ccel.org/ccel/bible/kjv.Sir.47
               .html>. Sirach, written between 100 BC and AD 100, is a book of
               wisdom found in the Apocrypha. See John Bowker, *The Complete
               Bible Handbook: An Illustrated Companion* (London: D.K. Publishing,
               1998), pp. 256-57.
Page 51   "earliest known narrative portrayal": "Panel from an ivory casket;
               the Crucifixion of Christ," The British Museum website (2008)
               <www.britishmuseum.org/explore/highlights/highlight_objects/
               pe_mla/p/panel_from_an_ivory_casket_th.aspx>.
Page 52   "The evidence is teasing": Colin Morris, *The Sepulchre of Christ and
               the Medieval West: From the Beginning to 1600* (New York: Oxford
               University Press, 2005), p. 32.

Chapter 8: The Man of Sorrows

Page 53   Lithuania is the home of: "Sacral Folk Art of Lithuania," Lithuanian Art
               Museum (2009) <www.ldm.lt/TDM/Sacral_folk_art_en.htm>.
Page 53   This word translates as: Lithuanian Mission Band website (2009)
               <www.cpprovince.org/archives/heritage/fall99/fall9913.php>.
Page 55   The art commentator describes Christ as: Annemarie Weyl Carr,
               "Double-Sided Icon with the Virgin Hodegetria and the Man of Sor-
               rows," in Annemarie Weyl Carr, *The Glory of Byzantium: Art and Cul-
               ture in the Middle Byzantine Era A.D. 843–1261* (New York: The Met-
               ropolitan Museum of Art and Harry N. Abrams, 1997), p. 125.
Page 56   The gospel writers repeatedly pointed out: See Matthew 9:36;
               14:14; 15:32; 20:34.

Chapter 9: Descent from the Cross

Page 59   hands clasped in a Byzantine expression of grief: Henry Maguire,
               "The Depiction of Sorrow in Middle Byzantine Art," *Dumbarton Oaks
               Papers,* vol. 31 (1977), p. 154.
Page 59   The sculpted marble figures divide: Rolf Toman, ed., *Romanesque: Archi-
               tecture, Sculpture, Painting* (Köln, Germany: Könemann, 1997), p. 305.

Chapter 10: Crucified with Christ

Page 64   Peter served as a missionary: "St. Peter, Prince of the Apostles,"
               Catholic Encyclopedia. New Advent website (2007) <www.newad
               vent.org/cathen/11744a.htm>.

Page 64   One of the first disciples called: "St. Andrew," *Catholic Encyclopedia,*
               New Advent website (2007) <www.newadvent.org/cathen/
               01471a.htm>.

Page 64   Bartholomew (sometimes identified as Nathanael): "St. Bartho-
               lomew," *Catholic Encyclopedia,* New Advent website (2007) <www
               .newadvent.org/cathen/02313c.htm>.

Page 65   "I have long desired this": John Kitto and Charles Hitchcock, *An Il-
               lustrated History of the Bible* (Norwich, Conn.: Henry Bill, 1869), p.
               624.

Page 65   "I am a Christian": "St. Blandina," *Catholic Encyclopedia,* New Advent
               website (2007) <www.new advent.org/cathen/025942a.htm>.

Page 65   "Blandina was filled with such power": John Lane, "St. Blandina and
               the Martyrs of Lyons," The Aquinas Site website (2008) <www
               .strobertbellarmine.net/saints/blandina.html>.

Page 66   "as if hanging on a cross": Ibid.

Pages 65-66   As one of the last martyrs: "St. Blandina," *Catholic Encyclopedia,* New
               Advent website (2007) <www.newadvent.org/cathen/025942a
               .htm>.

Page 66   Persecutors burned her body: "St. Blandina," Catholic Online web-
               site (2008) <www.catholic.org/saints/saint.php?saint_id=339>.

Page 66   "Whenever a man properly humbles": "Letters of Elder Macarius of
               Optina," St. Vladimir's website (2009) <www.stvladimirs.ca/
               library/elder-macarius-purity.html>.

Chapter 11: The Everywhere Cross

Page 68   As far as we know: Mary Beard and John Henderson, *Classical Art:
               From Greece to Rome* (New York: Oxford University Press, 2001), pp.
               237-38.

Page 69   "Our seals should be": Paul Corby Finney, *The Invisible God: The Ear-
               liest Christians on Art* (New York: Oxford University Press, 1994), p.
               111.

Page 70   Essentially, they kept the status quo: Ibid.

Page 70   But even before Clement's ring concerns: The anchor also repre-
               sented hope and steadfastness. The ship also symbolized the Church
               of Christ.

Page 70   Accordingly, archaeologists have found gems: Robin Margaret
               Jensen, *Understanding Early Christian Art* (New York: Routledge,
               2000), p. 138.

Page 70   "And, surely, your military ensigns": Ibid., p. 141.

Page 71   "For consider all the things": Philip Schaff, *The Apostolic Fathers with
               Justin Martyr and Irenaeus* (Grand Rapids: Eerdmans, 2001), n.p.

Christian Classics Ethereal Library website (2005) <www.ccel
.org/ccel/schaff/anf01.viii.ii.lv.html>.

Chapter 12: Graffiti Marks and Mocks

Page 73   paid homage to a hailed savior: Thomas F. Mathews, *The Clash of
               Gods* (Princeton, N.J.: Princeton University Press, 1993), pp. 48-
               59.

Page 73   "I hear that they": C. R. Haines, *The Correspondence of Marcus Corne-
               lius Fronto* (Cambridge, Mass.: Harvard University Press, 1982),
               n.p.

Page 74   "You know, they worship": T. R. Glover, *The Conflict of Religions in
               the Early Roman Empire* (Washington, D.C.: Cannon Press, 1974), p.
               212.

Page 74   "Everywhere they speak": Robert L. Wilken, *The Christians as the
               Romans Saw Them* (New Haven, Conn.: Yale University Press, 1984),
               p. 96.

Page 74   "But even if Christ had to suffer": Roger Pearse, ed., "Porphyry,
               Against the Christians Fragments," Tertullian.org website (2004)
               <www.tertullian.org/fathers/porphyry_against_christians_02_
               fragments.htm>.

Page 75   "For me the documents are": Glover, *Conflict of Religions in the Early
               Roman Empire,* p. 63.

Chapter 13: The Sign of Jonah

Page 78   Tourists might expect: Robin Margaret Jensen, *Understanding Early
               Christian Art* (New York: Routledge, 2000), p. 68.

Page 78   The story of Jonah wins: Ibid., p. 69.

Page 79   Origen taught three levels: Ibid., p. 77.

Page 80   The keepers of the catacombs of Saint Callixtus: "The Cubicles of
               Sacraments" (1997), The Catacombs of Saint Callixtus website
               <www.cata combe.roma.it/en/cal.html>.

Chapter 14: The Outstretched Hands

Page 82   It then became important: Robert Turcan, *The Gods of Ancient Rome*
               (New York: Routledge, 1998), p. 135.

Page 82   The Roman *Gemma Augustea*: The *Kunsthistorisches* Museum in Vi-
               enna, Austria, displays this cameo.

Page 83   The base of the Column of Antonius Pius: The *Apotheosis* of Anto-
               nius Pius and Faustina appear on the vase of the Column of Anto-
               nius Pius at the *Musei Vaticani* in Vatican City.

Page 83   A portrait bust of . . . Commodus: The Commodus as Hercules sculpture resides at the *Palazzo dei Conservatori* in Rome.

Page 83   In the first book: Turcan, *The Gods of Ancient Rome,* p. 2.

Page 83   "which god to invoke": Ibid.

Page 84   It's not always clear: Marilyn Stokstad, *Art History,* 3rd ed. (Upper Saddle River, N.J.: Pearson Prentice-Hall, 2008), p. 239.

Page 84   "the affectionate respect due": Robert Milburn, *Early Christian Art and Architecture* (Berkley: University of California Press, 1988), p. 32.

Page 84   "righteousness that exalts": Ibid.

Page 84   In 1955 at the site: G. Ernest Wright, "Hazor and the Conquest of Canaan," *The Biblical Archaeologist* 18, no. 4 (December 1955): 108.

Page 85   "We assuredly see the sign": David W. Bercot, ed., *A Dictionary of Early Christian Beliefs* (Peabody, Mass.: Hendrickson, 1998), p. 533.

Page 85   "We, however, not only raise": Philip Schaff, *Latin Christianity: Its Founder, Tertullian,* Christian Classics Ethereal Library website (2005) <www.ccel.org/ccel/schaff/anf03.vi.iv.xiv.html>.

Page 85   "With our hands thus stretched out": Bercot, ed., *Dictionary of Early Christian Beliefs,* p. 532.

Page 85   "He stretched out his arms": The Book of Common Prayer (Oxford: Oxford University Press, 1990), p. 362.

Chapter 15: Signs of the Cross

Page 87   the earliest known monastic: Thomas Bokenkotter, *A Concise History of the Catholic Church* (New York: Image Books), p. 50.

Page 87   "Believe me, Satan fears": Henry Borgman, *Libica: A Liturgical Biblical Catechetical Summary of the Catholic Religion* (Baltimore: Murphy, 1930), p. 42.

Page 88   Some sources believe Jesus: "The Sign of the Cross," Catholic Tradition website (2008) <www.catholictradition.org/Classics/signum crucis.htm>.

Page 88   Others say John the Evangelist: Ibid.

Page 88   the apostle Paul used it: Ibid.

Page 88   "The sign of the cross is the trophy": *Libica,* p. 232.

Page 88   "At every forward step": David W. Bercot, ed., *Dictionary of Early Christian Beliefs* (Peabody, Mass.: Hendrickson, 1998), p. 613.

Page 88   "Let us then not be ashamed to confess": Herbert Thurston, "Sign of the Cross," *Catholic Encyclopedia,* New Advent website <www.newadvent.org/cathen/06098b.htm>.

Page 88   "We Christians wear out our foreheads": Charles George Herbermann, *The Catholic Encyclopedia* (New York: The Encyclopedia Press, 1908), p. 520.

Page 88   However, Tertullian also revealed the practice: Herbert Thurston,

"Sign of the Cross," *Catholic Encyclopedia,* New Advent website <www.newadvent.org/cathen/06098b.htm>.

Page 89   "This is how it is done": Fr. William Saunders, "The Sign of the Cross," Catholic Education Resources Center Website (2003) <www.catholiceducation.org/articles/religion/re0129.html>.

Chapter 16: The Absent Crucifixion

Page 92   Although Christ's message: David Balch, "The Suffering of Isis/Io and Paul's Portrait of Christ Crucified (Gal. 3:1): Frescoes in the Pompeian and Roman Houses and the Temples of Isis in Pompeii," *Journal of Religion* 83 (2003): n.p.

Page 92   "Crucifixion was a punishment": Nigel Spivey, "Christ and the Art of Agony," *History Today* 99 (1999): 17.

Page 92   "The issue is not only": Robin Margaret Jensen, *Understanding Early Christian Art* (New York: Routledge, 2000), p. 134.

Page 93   "[It] has to do with public": Ibid.

Page 93   The sixth-century Rabbula Gospels: Henry Luttikhuizen and Dorothy Verkerk, *Snyder's Medieval Art* (Upper Saddle River, N.J.: Pearson, 2006), p. 46.

Page 93   "Not a symbolic sacrificial lamb": Marilyn Stokstad, *Medieval Art* (Boulder, Colo.: Westview, 2004), p. 180.

Chapter 17: The Emperor's Vision

Page 97   According to Eusebius, "[Constantine] said": The story and quotations about Constantine are from Philip Schaff and Henry Wallace, *Nicene and Post-Nicene Fathers, Volume 1* (New York: Cosimo, 2007), pp. 489-93.

Chapter 18: Searching for the Real Thing

Page 101   "she worshiped not the wood": Fr. William P. Saunders, "St. Helena and the True Cross," *Catholic Herald* website (2005) <www.catholicherald.com>.

Page 102   Constantine privately enclosed: Fernand Cabrol, "The True Cross," *The Catholic Encyclopedia* (2005), New Advent website <www.newadvent.org/cathen/04529a.htm>.

Page 102   In Jerusalem on Good Friday: Ibid.

Page 102   "He [Jesus] was truly crucified": Cyril of Jerusalem, "Lecture IV: On the Ten Points of Doctrine," Christian Classics Ethereal Library website (2005) <www.ccel.org/ccel/schaff/npnf207.ii.viii.html>.

Page 103   As early as the fourth century John Chrysostom noted: "The True Cross," *The Catholic Encyclopedia,* New Advent website (2005)

<www.newadvent.org/athen/04529a.htm>.

Page 103   In the fifth century, as a conciliatory gesture: Ibid.

Page 103   When Radegunda, Queen of the Franks: Ibid.

Page 103   In the ninth century Emperor Charlemagne: Magnus Backes and Regine Dölling, *Art of the Dark Ages* (New York: Harry N. Abrams, 1969), p. 70.

Page 103   "Fragments of the cross found": John Calvin, "Against the Worship of Relics," Christian Classics Ethereal Library website (2005), <www.ccel.org/ccel/schaff/hcc8.iv.xv.v.html>.

Page 104   "a greater controversy": Ibid.

Page 105   "It is written that the just": David W. Bercot, ed., *Dictionary of Early Christian Beliefs* (Peabody, Mass.: Hendrickson, 1998), p. 271.

Chapter 19: A Cross in the Desert

Page 106   A howling wind sweeps through the gorge: Descriptions of Saint Catherine's monastery and landscape are adapted from these sources: Iason Athanasiadis, "A Lily in the Desert," *Al-Ahram Weekly Online* 3-9, No. 567 (Jan. 2002), n.p. Available on *Al-Ahram Weekly* website (2002) <www.weekly.ahram.org.eg/2002/567/tr3.htm>. John Watson, "The Physical Components of the Monastery of Saint Catherine's in the Sinai of Egypt," Tour Egypt website (1999-2003) <www.touregypt.net/featurestories/catherines3.htm>. John Watson, "Gallery of Artifacts in the Monastery of St. Catherine Collection," Tour Egypt website (1999-2003) <www.touregypt.net/featurestories/catherines5.htm>. Helen C. Evans, *Saint Catherine's Monastery, Sinai, Egypt* (New York: The Metropolitan Museum of New York, 2004), pp. 11-19.

Page 107   Funded by Emperor Justinian in the sixth century:John Lowden, *Early Christian and Byzantine Art* (London: Phaidon, 1997), p. 74.

Page 107   A well-preserved icon known as the Sinai Christ: Henry Luttikhuizen and Dorothy Verkerk, *Snyder's Medieval Art* (Upper Saddle River, N.J.: Pearson, 2006), p. 71.

Page 108   Another icon, the Sinai Saint Peter: Ibid.

Page 108   His right hand holds silver keys: Mt 16:19.

Page 108   "The knowledge of the Cross is concealed": Monks of Holy Transfiguration Monastery, "One Hundred & Twenty Wise Sayings from The Holy Fathers of the Orthodox Church," The Balamand Monastery website, n.d. <www.balamandmonastery.org.lb/fathers/indexdesert.htm>.

Page 109   "Monasticism itself is a perpetual labor": Ibid.

Chapter 20: The Missionary Cross

Page 111   Reading the account of Columba's life: Columba's missionary activity was extensive and complicated. The stories touched on derive from these sources: Adamnan with William Reeves, ed., *Life of Saint Columba, Founder of Hy* (Edinburgh: Edmonston and Douglas, 1874). n.p. Posted as "Adamnan: Life of Saint Columba," Internet Medieval Sourcebook website (1998) <www.fordham.edu/halsall/basis/comuba-e.html>. Marilyn Stokstad, *Medieval Art* (Boulder, Colo.: Westview, 2004), p. 91.

Page 111   "to every cow its calf": Ibid.

Page 111   "I bind to myself today": This version of "The Lorica" is a literal translation from the Old Irish text from "Saint Patrick," New Advent website, n.d. <www.new advent.org/cathen/11554a.htm>.

Page 112   In the tradition of Columba and Patrick: Information about Celtic crosses derives from these sources: O. B. Duane, *Celtic Art* (London: Brockhampton Press, 1996), pp. 68-71. Henry Luttikhuizen and Dorothy Verkerk, *Snyder's Medieval Art* (Upper Saddle River, N.J.: Pearson, 2006), pp. 47-150; Marilyn Stokstad, *Art History,* 3rd ed. (Upper Saddle River, N.J.: Pearson Prentice-Hall, 2008), p. 449; Stokstad, *Medieval Art,* p. 93; Martin Werner, "On the Origin of the Form of the Irish High Cross," *Gesta* 29, no. 1 (1990): 98-110.

Page 113   "bearing a silver cross for their banner": Judith McClure and Roger Collins, eds., Bede, *The Ecclesiastical History of the English People* (New York: Oxford University Press, 1969), p. 40.

Page 113   "come from Rome, bearing the best:" Ibid., p. 39.

Chapter 21: Becoming More Christian

Page 114   I am agile of body: Arnold Talentino, "Riddle 30: The Vehicle of the Cross," *Neophilogolous* 65, no. 1 (January 1981): 129.

Page 115   An eighth-century slab in Aberlemno: Henry Luttikhuizen and Dorothy Verkerk, *Snyder's Medieval Art* (Upper Saddle River, N.J.: Pearson, 2006), pp. 149-50.

Page 115   In another curious mixture, the Papil Stone: Marilyn Stokstad, *Medieval Art* (Boulder, Colo.: Westview, 2004), p. 94.

Page 116   "King Harald had the memorial made": Marilyn Stokstad, *Art History,* 3rd ed. (Upper Saddle River, N.J.: Pearson Prentice-Hall, 2008), p. 460.

Page 116   Around this time in the British Isles: Ibid.

Page 117   These raids prompted a prayer for protection: Elise Rosenthal and David M. Wilson, eds. *From Viking to Crusader: The Scandinavians and Europe 800-122* (New York: Rizzoli, 1992), p. 80.

Chapter 22: A Cross for the Darkness

Page 122   However, pottery lamps didn't flourish: "Oil Lamps in the Ancient
                World," Ancient Lamps website (2009) <www.ancientlamps.com/
                ancientlamps.html>.

Page 122   Later, the Greeks innovated: Ibid.

Page 122   During the Hellenistic Age: Ibid.

Page 122   these popular *firmalampen:* W. V. Harris, "Roman Terra Cotta
                Lamps: The Organization of an Industry," *The Journal of Roman Stud-
                ies* 70 (1980): 127.

Page 123   The Herodian lamp: Robert Houston Smith, "The Household
                Lamps of Palestine in New Testament Times," *Biblical Archaeologist*
                29 (February 1966): 3-5.

Page 123   Pottery workshops in Cyrpus: Benjamin W. Porter, "Clay Lamps
                Shed New Light on Daily Life in Antiquity," *Near Eastern Archaeology*
                67, no. 3 (2004): 175.

Page 123   For example, researchers discovered: Ibid.

Page 124   "The mystery of the cross shines bright": Bill Swainson, *The Encarta
                Book of Quotations* (New York: St. Martin's Press, 2000), p. 345.

Chapter 23: Hoping for the Cross

Page 125   For example, a second-floor apartment in Herculaneum: Everett
                Ferguson, *Backgrounds of Early Christianity* (Grand Rapids: Eerdmans,
                2003), p. 590.

Page 126   Over the years scholars have ventured: Mary Rose Sheldon, "The
                Sator Rebus: An Unsolved Cryptogram?" *Cryptolgia* 27, no. 3 (July
                2003): 239-41.

Page 126   With closer inspection, some scholars deciphered: Ibid., p. 252.

Page 126   Equally compelling arguments pointed to: Duncan Fishwick, "On
                the Origin of the Rotas-Sator Square," *Harvard Theological Review* 57,
                no. 1 (1964): 39-53. Also see the footnotes in Ferguson, *Backgrounds
                of Early Christianity,* p. 590.

Page 127   It would have been spiritually and intellectually invigorating: For an
                early discussion, see Floyd V. Filson, "Were There Christians in
                Pompeii?" *The Biblical Archaeologist* 2, no. 2 (May 1939), pp. 13-16.

Page 127   Along with these controversial discoveries: Ferguson, *Backgrounds of
                Early Christianity,* p. 590.

Page 128   Jesus emphasized that when we search, we will find: Mt 7:7.

Chapter 24: Fear No Evil

Page 129   "Christ wins, Christ reigns": Yael Israeli and David Mevorah, eds.,
                Cradle of Christianity (Jerusalem: The Israel Museum, 2000), p. 127.

Page 130   An amulet is "an object that by its nearness": Everett Ferguson, *Backgrounds of Early Christianity* (Grand Rapids: Eerdmans, 2003), p. 233.

Page 130   In the fourth century the presbyter Basil of Caesarea: Vasiliki Limberi, "The Eyes Infected by Evil: Basil of Caesarea's Homily, 'On Envy,'" *Harvard Theological Review* 84, no. 2 (April 1991): 163. Most of evil-eye discussion in this chapter depends on the information in this article.

Page 130   "For thus it is. The Scythian does not cast the evil eye": Ibid., p. 174.

Page 130   For over a millennium eastern Mediterranean cultures: Ibid., p. 175.

Page 131   "If you strive for the [proper] glory": Ibid., p. 181.

Chapter 25: The Trustworthy Standard

Page 133   This scale "consisted of a beam": Ronald F. Youngblood, ed., *Nelson's New Illustrated Bible Dictionary* (Nashville: Thomas Nelson, 1995), pp. 1307-8.

Page 134   Bronze weights with crosses promised fairness and honesty: Yael Israeli and David Mevorah, eds., *Cradle of Christianity* (Jerusalem: The Israel Museum, 2000), pp. 127, 138.

Page 135   For example, a circa fifth- to sixth-century bronze weight: Ibid., pp. 138, 222.

Page 135   a copy of the Byzantine *Homilies of Gregory Nazianzus:* "Use of Coins," Dumbarton Oaks Research Library and Collection website (2008), <www.doaks.org/CoinExhibition/Introduction/Frame_Introduction.html>.

Page 135   Like the boxed Roman weights-and-scale set: Sir W. M. Flinders Petri, *Glass Stamps and Weights: Ancient Weights and Measures* (Encino, Calif.: Malter, 1974), pp. 26, 42, xvi.

Page 135   The Scales of Justice: Thomas V. Vincent, "Answer to Question about the Origin of Lady of Justice," Legal History and Philosophy by Thomas V. Vincent (2000-2001) <www.commonlaw.com/Justice.html>.

Page 135   A fourth- to fifth-century *amphora*: Alexander Minchev, "Unusual Christian Stamp on Early Byzantine Amphora-Neck from Varna," International Round Table: Production and Trade of Amphorae in the Black Sea website (2006) <www.patabs.org>.

Chapter 26: Coins for the Kingdom

Page 137   It's possible to trace the lineage of Roman and Byzantine emperors:

For a fascinating history of Byzantine coins, visit "Bearers of Meaning: The Otillia Buerger Collection of Ancient and Byzantine Coins at Lawrence University," Lawrence University website (1996) <www.lawrence.edu/dept/art/buerger/intro/contents.html>.

Page 137   "The use of coins welds together our whole life": Kenneth W. Harl, *Coinage in the Roman Economy, 300 B. C. to A. D. 700* (Baltimore: Johns Hopkins University Press, 1996), p. 250.

Page 138   "One important legacy of Constantine's authority": "Silver argenteus of Constantine the Great," The British Museum webite, n.d. <www.britishmuseum.org/explore/highlights/highlight_objects/cm/silver_argenteus_of_Constantine.aspx>.

Page 138   A silver coin from the beginning: Ibid.

Page 138   distributed a golden coin: "Gold medallion showing Constantine the Great at prayer," The British Museum Website, n.d. <www.britishmuseum.org/explore/highlights/highlight_objects/cm/g/gold_medallion_showing_constan.aspx>.

Page 138   A third coin at the British Museum: "Bronze nummus of Magnentius with Christogram," The British Museum Website, n.d. <www.britishmuseumorgexplorehighlightshighlight_objects/cm/b/bronze_nummus_of_magnentius_wi.aspx>.

Page 139   coins adopted an "overtly Christian character": Introduction, Coinage of the Byzantine Empire Exhibit, Dumbartor Oaks Research Library and Collection website (2000) <www.doaks.org/Coin Exhibition/Introduction/Frame_Introduction.html>.

Page 139   Byzantine rulers imprinted coins: Ibid.

Chapter 27:   Walking the Cross

Page 143   I heard that early Christians devoted themselves to fellowship: Acts 2:42; 5:42.

Page 143   By the early fourth century Christians worshiped in halls: John Lowden, *Early Christian & Byzantine Art* (London: Phaidon 1997), pp. 18-21.

Page 144   "The modest buildings and houses": Marilyn Stokstad, *Medieval Art* (Boulder, Colo.: Westview, 2004), p. 23.

Page 144   architects modeled the first "official" churches after a structure: Marilyn Stokstad, *Art History,* 3rd ed. (Upper Saddle River, N.J.: Pearson Prentice-Hall, 2008), pp. 205-6.

Page 145   Peter, the "rock" on whom Jesus built his church: Mt 16:18.

Page 146   "It is the doors that admit us:" Romano Guardini, *Sacred Signs* (St. Louis, Mo.: Pio Decimo, 1956), pp. 39-40.

Chapter 28: Follow Me

Page 147   Early church ordines: "Procession," *Encyclopedia Britannica 1911* website (2006) <www.1911encyclopedia.org/Procession>.

Page 148   A hymn in honor of the cross: Glanville Downey, "A Processional Cross," *The Metropolitan Museum of Art Bulletin, New Series* 12, no. 9 (May 1954): 276.

Page 148   Before the age of Constantine: "Processions," The Original Catholic Encyclopedia website (2007) <www.oce.catholic.com/index .php?title=Processions>.

Page 148   Small engravings on the cross: Yael Israeli and David Mevorah, eds., *Cradle of Christianity* (Jerusalem: The Israel Museum, 2000), p. 90.

Pages 148-9   In the tenth century the Visigoth King: Magnus Backes and Regine Dölling, *Art of the Dark Ages* (New York: Harry N. Abrams, 1969), pp. 249-51.

Page 149   The twelfth-century Cross of Cong: O. B. Duane, *Celtic Art* (London: Brockhampton Press, 1996), pp. 75-7.

Page 149   "Give me chastity and continence": Clifton Fadiman, ed., *The Little, Brown Book of Anecdotes* (Boston: Little, Brown and Co., 1985), p. 5.

Page 150   Clement of Rome explained: David W. Bercot, ed., *A Dictionary of Early Christian Beliefs* (Peabody, Mass.: Hendrickson, 1998), p. 579.

Page 150   "If we follow this way": Dietrich Bonhoeffer, *The Cost of Discipleship* (New York: Macmillan, 1961), pp. 211-12.

Chapter 29: The Cross and the Water

Page 151   Some of the oldest cross fonts: Yael Israeli and David Mevorah, eds., *Cradle of Christianity* (Jerusalem: The Israel Museum, 2000), p. 61.

Page 152   "Onward he presses, to the passion": Nathan D. Mitchell, "Washed Away by the Blood of God," in *The Cross in Christian Tradition,* ed. Elizabeth A. Dryer (New York: Paulist Press, 2000), p. 60.

Page 152   By the fourth century, this preparation divided into four parts: "Catechumen," *Catholic Encyclopedia,* New Advent website (2007) <www.newadvent.org/cathen/03430b.htm>.

Page 153   "followed by the making of the sign of the cross": Ibid., p. 37.

Page 153   The salt symbolized: Pope Pius V, *Catechism of the Council of Trent* (Baltimore: Lucas Brothers, 1829), p. 134.

Page 153   Names must be given in before the first day of Lent: Robert Louis Wilken, *The Spirit of Early Christian Thought* (New Haven, Conn.: Yale University Press, 2003), pp. 37-38.

Page 153   At the fourth-century Church of Moses on Mount Nebo: *Cradle of Christianity,* p. 66.

Page 154   Clement of Alexandria explained this enlightenment: David W.
                Bercot, ed., *A Dictionary of Early Christian Beliefs* (Peabody, Mass.:
                Hendrickson, 1998), p. 52.
Page 154   For example, in the fifth century at the Byzantine Basilica: Israeli
                and Mevorah, eds., *Cradle of Christianity*, pp. 66-67.
Page 154   the freshly baptized drank a cup of milk and honey: Edward En-
                gelbrecht, "God's Milk: An Orthodox Confession of the Eucharist,"
                Journal of Early Christian Studies 7, no. 4 (Winter 1999), n.p.
Page 155   "Blessed are they who, placing their trust": Bercot, ed., *Dictionary of
                Early Christian Beliefs*, p. 51.

Chapter 30: Breaking the Bread
Page 156   Historians believe these bakeries with their huge ovens: Dr. Joanne
                Berry, "Work and Play in Everyday Pompeii Gallery," BBC website
                (2009)   <www.bbc.co.uk/history/ancient/romans/daily_life_
                gallery_02.shtml>.
Pages 156-57   Christians donated bread to the church: Yael Israeli and David Me-
                vorah, eds., *Cradle of Christianity* (Jerusalem: The Israel Museum,
                2000), p. 97.
Page 157   He was born in Bethlehem, which means "house of bread": H. E.
                Jacob, *Six Thousand Years of Bread* (New York: Lyons Press, 1944),
                p. 91.
Page 157   "Therefore, the people asked one question of each new prophet":
                Ibid., p. 93.
Page 159   Early liturgies from the first through the fourth centuries: Rev.
                George Mastrantonis, "Introduction to the Divine Liturgy," Greek
                Orthodox Archdiocese of America website (2009) <www.goarch
                .org/ourfaith/ourfaith7117>.
Page 159   He recited, "Having beheld the resurrection of Christ": "The Pas-
                chal Hours," Orthodox.net website (2009) <www.orthodox.net/
                pascha/paschal-hours-dblsided-2perside.rtf>.

Chapter 31: Take This Cup
Page 161   Finally, in the twentieth century: "The Antioch Chalice," The Met-
                ropolitan Museum website (2000-2008) <www.metmuseum.org/
                toah/ho/06/waa/ho_50.4.htm>.
Page 162   "one of the most splendid treasures of the Middle Ages": "Chalice of
                the Abbot Suger of Saint-Denis," National Gallery of Art website
                (2009) <www.nga.gov/collection/gallery/medieval-1437.html>.
Page 162:   Some of the most famous chalices: Noteworthy Eucharist cups
                without crosses created before the first millennium include the

eighth-century Ardagh Chalice in the National Museum of Ireland; the Tassilo Chalice at the Kremsmünster Abbey in Austria, also from the eighth century; the tenth-century Saint Gauzelin Chalice at the Cathedral of Nancy in France; and the tenth-century Chalice of Emperor Romanos II at the Treasury of San Marco in Italy.

Page 162   "I am the Alpha and Omega": Ibid.

Page 162   "Treasure of St. Sergios": "Chalice with Apostles Venerating the Cross," The Walters Art Museum website (2009) <www.art.the walters.org/viewwoa.aspx?id=9463>.

Chapter 32: Decorating the Sacred

Page 164   These light sources, crafted in silver and niello: "Cross-Shaped Polycandelon," Dumbarton Oaks Research Library and Collection website (2008) <www.museum.doaks.org/OBJ?sid=837&rec=29 &page=29>.

Page 165   Although divided into separate exhibitions: The Sion Treasure objects reside at the Dumbarton Oaks Research Library in Washington, D.C., the Antalya Museum in Turkey and a few private collections.

Page 165   "a multilayered surface that is highly animated": "Silver Paten with Christogram and Repoussé Border," Dumbarton Oaks Research Library and Collection website (2008) <www.museum.doaks.org/ OBJ?sid=501&rec=2&page=2>.

Page 166   However, the humble artifacts teach us: These objects appear in Yael Israeli and David Mevorah, eds., *Cradle of Christianity* (Jerusalem: The Israeli Museum, 2000), pp. 54, 69, 89, 98, 104-5.

Page 166   "We ask not of you, O Father": Cindy Crosby ed. and Thomas C. Oden, general ed., *Ancient Christian Devotional* (Downers Grove, Ill.: InterVarsity Press, 2007), p. 237.

Chapter 33: The Iconoclastic Clash

Page 168   In the seventh century a Christian woman: John Lowden, *Early Christian & Byzantine Art* (London: Phaidon, 1997), p. 149.

Page 170   "What writing presents to readers": *Understanding Early Christian Art,* pp. 2-3.

Page 171   For example, in the council of chambers: Lowden, *Early Christian & Byzantine Art,* pp. 163-64.

Chapter 34: Pilgrims of the Cross

Page 175   "see, touch, and breathe the air": Yael Israeli and David Mevorah, eds., *Cradle of Christianity* (Jerusalem: The Israel Museum, 2000), p. 190.

Page 176   "in adoration before the cross": Jonathan Sumption, *Pilgrimage* (To-
            towa, N.J.: Rowman & Littlefield, 1975), p. 91.

Page 176   Egeria, a nun from Spain or Southern Gaul: Diana Webb, *Medieval
            European Pilgrimage* (New York: Palgrave, 2002), p. 3.

Page 176   "For it was always customary": M. L. McClure and C. L. Feltoe,
            ed. and trans., *The Pilgrimage of Etheria* (London: SPCK, 1919), p.
            20.

Page 177   "lifeless spots where the saints had lived": "Pilgrimage," *Catholic En-
            cyclopedia,* New Advent website (2007) <www.newadvent.org/
            cathen/12085a.htm>.

Page 177   "a place, far on the eastern side": G. R. Evans, *Faith in the Medi-
            eval World* (Downers Grove, Ill.: InterVarsity Press, 2002), p.
            140.

Page 177   "to cross the seas": "Pilgrimage," *Catholic Encyclopedia,* New Advent
            website (2007) <www.newadvent.org/cathen/12085a.htm>.

Page 177   "There were several Samaritan cities": Gary Vikan, *Byzantine Pilgrimage
            Art* (Washington, D.C.: Dumbarton Oaks Center for Byzantine Studies,
            1982), p. 7.

Page 178   "They offer oil to be blessed": Israeli and Mevorah, eds., *Cradle of
            Christianity,* p. 201.

Page 178   "There are ornaments in vast numbers": Vikan, *Byzantine Pilgrimage
            Art,* p. 10.

Chapter 35: The Ecumenical Cross

Page 180   "Ireland had few walls and divided pastures": Tim Bond, "The De-
            velopment of Christian Society in Early England, Part 3," in "The
            Church: Past and Present," Britannia Internet Magazine website
            (1998) <www.britannia.com/church/bond3.html>.

Page 181   "Cuthbert was a perfect choice": David Ross, "Saint Cuthbert,"
            Britain Express website (2006) <www.britainexpress.com/His
            tory/saxon/cuthbert.htm>.

Page 182   "The making of the Lindisfarne Gospels is different": Michelle P.
            Brown, "The Lindisfarne Gospels," Fathom website, Session 2, n.d.
            <www.fathom.com/course/33702501/session2.html>.

Page 183   "Embedded within [the carpet page]": Michele P. Brown, "The
            Lindisfarne Gospels," Fathom website, Session 4, n.d. <www
            .fathom.com/course/33702501/session4.html>.

Page 183   "You could tell a Pict, a Copt": "The Lindisfarne Gospels Tour:
            Meaning to Society," The British Library website (2009) <www
            .bl.uk/onlinegallery/features/lindisfarne/society.html>.

Chapter 36: Desperately Seeking Sanctuary

Page 184   "greatest Norman building in England": "Welcome to Durham Ca-
            thedral," Durham Cathedral website (2006-2008) <www.durham
            cathedral.co.uk>.

Page 184   The runaway banged on the cathedral's north door: Debra Shipley,
            Durham Cathedral (London: Tauris Parke Books, 1990), p. 27.

Page 185   If anyone in the realm violated: "Sanctuary," *Catholic Encyclopedia*
            (2008) <www.newadvent.org/cathen/13430a.htm>.

Page 185   Once inside, the criminal confessed: Shipley, *Durham Cathedral*, p.
            27.

Page 185   If a criminal chose to "quit the kingdom": Philip Clucas, *England's
            Churches* (Guilford, U.K.: Colour Library Books, 1984), p. 133.

Page 185   In Egyptian, Greek, and Roman temples, the *cella:* "Sanctuary," *Lu-
            minarium Encyclopedia* website (1996-2007) <www.luminarium
            .org/encyclopedia/sanctuary.htm>.

Page 185   The earliest written documentation: "The Anglo-Saxon Dooms,
            560-975," Internet Medieval Sourcebook website (1998) <www
            .fordham.edu/halsall/source560-975dooms.html>.

Page 186   the fugitive needed to sit on a *frith:* "Sanctuary," *Catholic Encyclopedia*
            (2008) <www.newadvent.org/cathen/13430a.htm>.

Page 186   Norman kings legislated two kinds of sanctuary churches: Ibid.

Page 186   Over time, a court poet: "Sanctuary," Classic Encyclopedia/
            Love to Know 1911 website (2006) <www.1911encyclopedia.org/
            Sanctuary>.

Page 186   Stone crosses inscribed: Ibid.

Page 186   In eleventh-century Scotland: Ibid.

Page 187   His love for humanity flows deeper and wider than we can imagine:
            Rom 8:39. So does his mercy: Eph 2:4-5.

Chapter 37: Hearts Up

Page 188   "[This piece] consolidates": Thomas F. Mathews, "The Fieschi Mor-
            gan Reliquary," in *The Glory of Byzantium: Art and Culture in the Middle
            Byzantine Era A.D. 843–1261* (New York: The Metropolitan Museum
            of Art and Harry N. Abrams, 1997), p. 74.

Page 189   "Christ descended into hell": Ibid.

Page 189   "Bishop: The Lord be with you": Hippolytus *Church Order* 31.11.21,
            ed. F. X. Funk (New York: Cambridge University Press, 1956), pp.
            524-25.

Chapter 38: The Veiled Cross

Page 191   Taken from the *Regularis Concordia:* Adolphus Ward and William

Trent, et al., "The Early Religious Drama," *The Drama to 1642, Part One, Vol. 5* of The Cambridge History of English and American Literature in 18 Volumes (New York: G.P. Putnam's Sons, 1907–1921), pp. 1-3.

Page 191   Many scholars believe the roots: Nathan D. Mitchell, "The Cross That Spoke," in *The Cross in Christian Tradition*, p. 75.

Page 192   According to instructions in the *Regularis Concordia*: Ibid.

Page 192   The *Regularis Concordia* directed: Aethelwold, Bishop of Winchester, *Monastic Agreement of the Monks and Nuns of the English Nation*, trans. Thomas Symons (New York: Oxford University Press, 1953), p. 43.

Page 193   "the holy Cross shall be guarded": Ibid., pp. 44-45.

Page 193   "Come and see the place": Andrew Sofer, "Absorbing Interests: Kyd's Bloody Handkerchief as Palimpsest," *Comparative Drama* (June 2000), n.p.

Page 193   "take up the shroud and spread it": Ibid.

Page 194   "We glory in your cross, O Lord": "Anthem 1, Good Friday," The Book of Common Prayer, p. 281.

Chapter 39: The Eternal Kingdom

Page 195   "Long life and victory to Charles": Derek Wilson, *Charlemagne* (New York: Doubleday, 2006), p. 81.

Page 196   "When God elected ninety-nine kingdoms": Robert Morrissey, *Charlemagne and France: A Thousand Years of Mythology*, trans. Catherine Tihanyi (Notre Dame, Ind.: University of Notre Dame Press, 2003), p. 58.

Page 197   Voltaire looked back and cynically quipped: Angela Partington, ed., *The Oxford Dictionary of Quotations* (New York: Oxford University Press, 1996), p. 716.

Page 198   the first shall be last: Mt 19:30; childlike faith: Lk 18:17; and it's hard for a rich person: Mt 19:24; the kingdom of God is near: Lk 10:9; willingness to repent: Mk 1:15; kingdom to live within us: Lk 17:21.

Chapter 40: To Rise Again

Page 199   If a strong wind sweeps: Information about the Hill of Crosses from Gordon McLachlan, *Lithuania* (Guilford, Conn.: Globe Pequot Press, 2002), pp. 222-23.

Page 202   A burial cave near: Joan E. Taylor, *Christians and the Holy Places* (Oxford: Oxford University Press, 1993), pp. 9-10.

About the Author

Judith Couchman is an award-winning author who has published more than forty books and compilations. She teaches art history part time at the University of Colorado at Colorado Springs, and also works as a speaker and writing coach. Judith holds a B.S. in education (English and journalism), an M.A. in journalism, and an M.A. in art history. She lives in Colorado Springs, Colorado.

Visit Judith's website, blogs, and other online addresses at the following: <www.judithcouchman.com>; <www.judithcouchman.blogspot.com>; <www.startingover-judithcouchman.blogspot.com>; <www.facebook.com>; <www.twitter.com>.

Works by Judith Couchman

The Art of Faith

The Mystery of the Cross

The Shadow of His Hand

Daring to Be Different for God
(Deborah)

Becoming a Woman God Can Use
(Esther)

Entrusting Your Dreams to God
(Hannah)

Choosing the Joy of Obedience (Mary)

A Garden's Promise

Celebrating Friendship

His Gentle Voice

Designing a Woman's Life Workbook

The Woman Behind the Mirror

Shaping a Woman's Soul

Designing a Woman's Life

Lord, Have You Forgotten Me?

Lord, Please Help Me to Change

Why Is Her Life Better Than Mine?

If I'm So Good, Why Don't I Act That Way?

Getting a Grip on Guilt

Compilations

Amazing Grace

The Encouraging Psalm

Encouragement for the Heart

Voices of Faith

Promises for Spirit-Led Living

Growing in Grace

His Redeeming Love

The Way of Faith

Called to Commitment

Cherished Thoughts about Friendship

Cherished Thoughts about Love

Cherished Thoughts about Prayer

The Promise of Power

Breakfast for the Soul

One Holy Passion

This One Thing I Do

For Me to Live Is Christ

Growing Deeper with God

Anywhere He Leads Me

Dare to Believe

A Very Present Help

Loving God with All Your Heart

Contributor

Life Promises Bible

Women of Faith Bible

formatio
TRADITION. EXPERIENCE.
TRANSFORMATION.

Formatio books from InterVarsity Press follow the rich tradition of the church in the journey of spiritual formation. These books are not merely about being informed, but about being transformed by Christ and conformed to his image. Formatio stands in InterVarsity Press's evangelical publishing tradition by integrating God's Word with spiritual practice and by prompting readers to move from inward change to outward witness. InterVarsity Press uses the chambered nautilus for Formatio, a symbol of spiritual formation because of its continual spiral journey outward as it moves from its center. We believe that each of us is made with a deep desire to be in God's presence. Formatio books help us to fulfill our deepest desires and to become our true selves in light of God's grace.